Explaining Metals Prices

ROCHESTER STUDIES IN ECONOMICS
AND POLICY ISSUES

Series Editor: Karl Brunner
University of Rochester, USA

Other titles in the series:

Controlling the Growth of Monetary Aggregates, by
Robert H. Rasche and James M. Johannes

Privatization and State-Owned Enterprise: Lessons from the United States, Great Britain and Canada, by
Paul W. MacAvoy, William T. Stanbury, George K. Yarrow, and
Richard H. Zeckhauser

Published in cooperation with

The Bradley Policy Research Center
William E. Simon Graduate School of
Business Administration
University of Rochester
Rochester, New York

Explaining Metals Prices

Economic Analysis of Metals Markets in the 1980s and 1990s

Paul W. MacAvoy
Dean and John M. Olin Professor
of Public Policy and Business Administration
William E. Simon Graduate School of Business Administration
University of Rochester

Kluwer Academic Publishers
Boston/Dordrecht/London

Distributors

for North America: Kluwer Academic Publishers,
101 Philip Drive, Assinippi Park, Norwell, MA 02061, USA

for the UK and Ireland: Kluwer Academic Publishers,
Falcon House, Queen Square, Lancaster LA1 1RN, UK

for all other countries: Kluwer Academic Publishers Group,
Distribution Centre, P. O. Box 322, 300 AH Dordrecht,
The Netherlands

Library of Congress Cataloging-in-Publication Data

MacAvoy, Paul W.
Explaining metals prices / Paul W. MacAvoy.
p. cm. — (Rochester studies in economics and policy issues)
"Published in cooperation with The Bradley Policy Research Center,
William E. Simon Graduate School of Business Administration.
University of Rochester, New York."
Includes index.
ISBN-13: 978-94-010-7712-5 e-ISBN-13: 978-94-009-2687-5
DOI: 10.1007/978-94-009-2687-5

1. Metals—Prices—Mathematical models. I. Bradley Policy
Research Center. II. Title. III. Series.
HD9506.A2M285 1988
338.2'3—dc19 88-23138
CIP

Softcover reprint of the hardcover 1st edition 1988

CONTENTS

TABLES AND CHARTS

List of Tables

Tables (continued)

List of Charts

PREFACE

Work on this book began in the Spring of 1983, not long after an Amax Corporation annual budget meeting. As a member of the Amax board of directors since 1979, I had been present at such meetings in which the molybdenum price had been forecast to move higher than $7.00 per pound. The actual annual average prices were $9.70 in 1980, $8.50 in 1981, and $4.00 in 1982. The forecast for 1983 called for prices to return to higher levels, but as both dealer and producer prices declined further, my research began in earnest.

Initially, the research was to address the question of why the molybdenum price had declined by more than half in a short period. More fundamental, as other metals prices also declined, was an impelling need to know the causes of the abrupt and sustained reduction in metals price levels that year. As prices stayed at low levels, while those of other materials recovered over the 1983-1986 period, the question became that of why metals prices had remained at startlingly low levels for over five years.

My intent has been to provide a consistent framework within which to provide answers. My first step "explains" the reduced price levels of the early 1980s by specifying price level equations that fit the historical price series and contain all the important causal variables. In a second step, I undertake "predictions" of price levels for some future years (after taking into consideration expected changes in determining variables).

Prices are annual averages of producer and dealer prices for as many of the major metals as it's been possible to compile 20-year series. These are the prices put on the overhead projectors at the annual planning sessions of corporate boards. Thus this research centers on explaining and predicting annual average prices for seven metals in the 1980s and early 1990s.

As work progressed, I was fortunate to be able to present early findings to many groups in the metals industry. Frequent presentations to the Amax Board has provided the basis for substantial evaluation of progress. In particular, explaining to that Board both the rise and fall of molybdenum prices in the preceding ten years has been difficult--and very rewarding.

The results here focus on "price level equations" that describe annual price averages over the 1960-1986 period for both individual metals and groups of metals. Based on the theories of economists and metals specialists, the equations were formulated to achieve maximum explainability as defined in statistical methodology. As the equations developed, they were affected by data limitations. Data series for 1960-1986 were constructed for fitting equations containing six variables. Since this data set had not been constructed previously, various series were incomplete at most of the stages of the research; series on capacity, and on inventories held by buyers, were never completed. The explanatory equations were therefore less complete than if the inventories, production and capacity of various metals had been known.

When this equation formulation was presented, the response of some experts was that it was all wrong. Their view was that the price level was not in equilibrium and for that reason could not be affected by supply-and-demand changes. They believed, rather, that the price level was still moving downward in a process of disequilibrium determined by current and past price reductions. This argument was expressed by them often enough to be taken seriously. Their implication that the level of price was not explainable commanded attention. The argument that prices were in dynamic disequilibrium thus became the alternative hypothesis for explaining the sustained collapse of prices.

The final result of this analysis is a set of alternative working price level equations, any one of which explains approximately four fifths of the variation in prices during the periods of successive increases of the 1970s and successive decreases of the 1980s. The analysis, in rejecting theories of a destabilizing process, reaffirms the central roles of inventories, exchange rates and final goods production in an equilibrating process for finding a stable price level. Applying the price level equations, the chief finding is that prices will not likely return to 1970s levels. Structural changes, particularly from the outbreak of competition in nickel and molybdenum, and perhaps in aluminum, have created permanently lower prices for the principal metals. This provides only limited optimism for the planning sessions in the board room.

This study has been a project of the Bradley Policy Research Center of the William E. Simon Graduate School of Business Administration. The assistance of Olin Fellows Taj Bindra, Harin deSilva, Patricia Gray and Betsy Nichols is gratefully acknowledged. Professor Hendrik Houthakker at Harvard, and Professors Raymond Ball, Thomas Cooley and Jerold Zimmerman at Rochester, all provided detailed comments on the early versions of the manuscript that were very beneficial. Three anonymous readers for publication are acknowledged for their positive criticisms of the manuscript draft.

The suggestions and, indeed, the hypotheses provided by Alan Born, Harold Brown, John DuCane, Pierre Gousseland and Michael Simeon, all of Amax Corporation, were seminal to the development of this project. Would that they and others making decisions based on metals prices could abide the results.

Chapter One

THE METALS PRICE COLLAPSE OF THE EARLY 1980s

During the 1970s, metals prices increased at least at the rate of inflation, and in some years in increments that heightened general inflationary expectations. But from 1980 to 1986 this linkage was broken. Metals prices declined while general price indices worldwide continued to increase. Chart One illustrates the reversal: The price indices for six out of seven important metals rose more rapidly than the wholesale price index before 1980, but for all seven metals the indices were at or below the wholesale price index throughout the first six years of this decade. Moreover, the relationship of metals prices and the business cycle was severed. The "collapse" of the prices of metals, relative to those of other goods and services, took place over both the 1980 and 1982 recessions, and also during the sustained expansion of the world economy from 1982 to 1987.

The collapse in the 1980-1987 period resulted in absolutely lower current dollar prices for four metals. Molybdenum prices decreased the most, by 66 percent, on producer sales between the major producers and the large buyers using the metal as an additive in steel production. Copper prices fell by more than 40 percent through the 1980-1986 period, and were still 20 percent lower than in 1980--even after substantial one-year increases in 1987. Lead prices fell 16 percent on producer sales in the same period. Nickel prices were down only six percent on contracts, but fell by almost one third on sales by dealers to small and large buyers in the dealer market from 1980 to 1987.

The three metals that experienced some current dollar price appreciation were aluminum, steel and zinc. The increase for each was less than half the rate of inflation (see Chart One). The aluminum and zinc price increases affected smaller volumes of producer sales, as demand shifted to the dealer markets (dealer prices for aluminum declined, and those for zinc remained constant over the time period). Carbon steel prices on producer sales increased by one third from 1980 to 1985, but by the end of 1987 had fallen back by 11 percent from the 1985 high.

What caused metals prices to decline or stagnate during a period in which other prices continued to increase? Numerous explanations can be found in the industry trade press. Excess capacity and inventories have been given the credit in some individual metals markets, while new technologies that require less metals utilization have been cited as the cause in other cases.[1] But the phenomenon of relative price decline encompassed all the metals, leading to the inference that there were common causal factors.

The factors driving down prices can be divided into two classes--although making such a demarcation risks over-simplification. The first class consists of those factors leading to increases in supply and decreases in demand which, when

---

[1]Specifically, excess inventories have been alleged to have affected molybdenum prices. In 1982 there was enough molybdenum in worldwide stocks that without any production during that year, demand could have been met ("Nickel Capacity May Last Remainder of Decade," *American Metals Market*, 16 December 1982). This excess inventory continued through 1984; year-end producer stocks of molybdenum amounted to about an 11-month supply (U.S. Bureau of Mines, *1986 Minerals Yearbook*, preprint [Washington, D.C., 1987], 3).

With respect to metals utilization, for copper purchasers the "higher, more volatile prices of the previous decade had acted as a catalyst to define new and more efficient processes. . . The copper-consuming industries that remained worked diligently to reduce costs through re-engineering of products and elimination of waste and usage" ("Understanding the Copper Market," *American Metals Market*, 29 April 1988).

Chart One. Producer Metals Prices, 1960 - 1986.

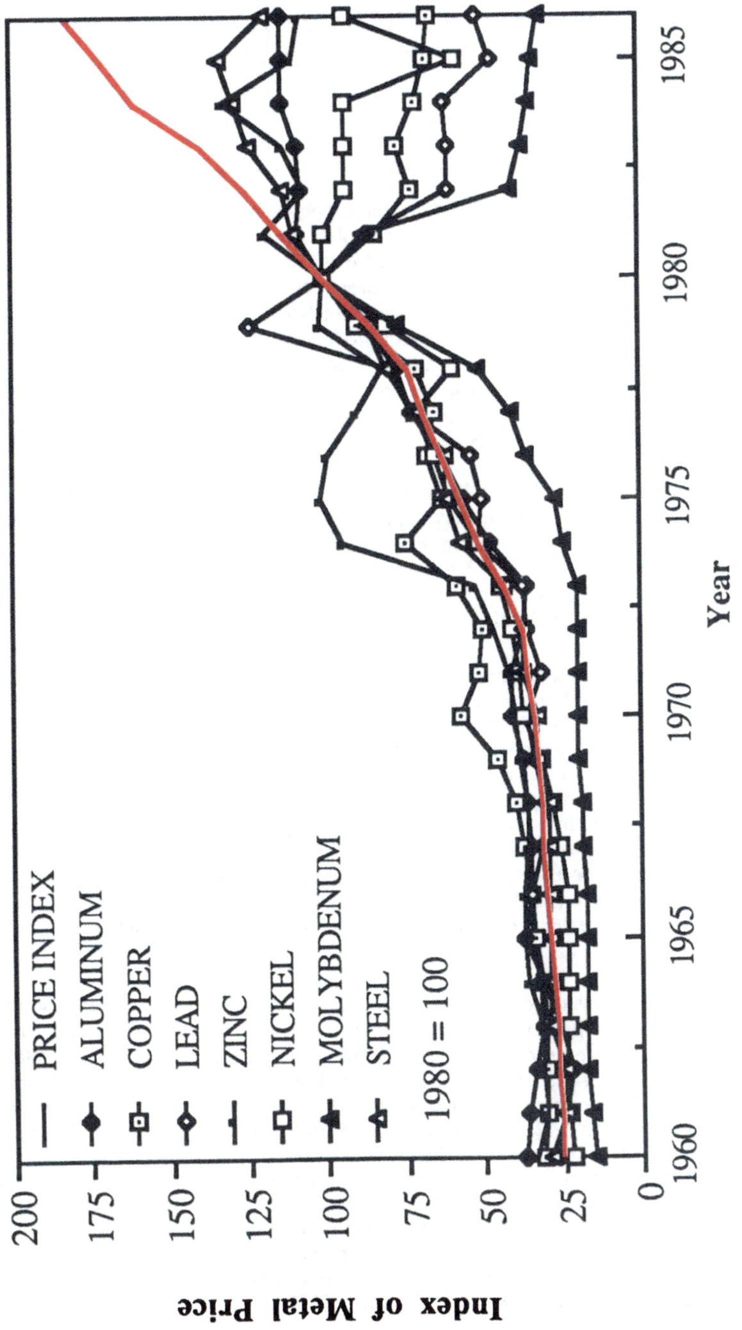

working through markets, cause lower equilibrium prices.[2] The second is made up of disequilibrating practices of producers or consumers based on powerful speculative and political motives.[3] These practices work on the market to destabilize prices, and it

---

[2]The trade press frequently outlines the supply-demand process as the means for effecting price changes. One early and relatively complete rendition is found in the article "Dark Days for Nonferrous Metals," in which *Chemical Week* attributes the low metals prices to declining demands and increasing supplies. The article states that "the worldwide plunge in demand is coming at the same time as increased competition from outside the U.S." The 'worldwide plunge in demand' is attributed to the decline in production of metals goods in the leading industrial nations. For example the copper industry had 90 percent of its market tied to such cyclical industries as construction, power generation and transmission, and machinery and transportation equipment production, and these industries were experiencing a recession at the time. Technological substitution of metals also contributed to the decline in demand: Zinc was competing strongly with engineering plastics for what little demand was left. Demand for lead declined as a result of longer-life batteries and environmental restrictions on lead levels in gasoline. The increase in metals supplies was attributed to "newly tapped resources in undeveloped nations." As President Frank Joklit of Kennecott Minerals said, "There is nothing basically wrong with the copper business that isn't wrong with the economy as a whole . . . When people ask me, 'When will the copper business turn up?' I say, 'When will the economy turn up?'" ("Dark Days for Nonferrous Metals," *Chemical Week*, 14 July 1982: 36-42).

[3]The trade press attributes price volatility to the speculative nature of dealer and futures markets, such as the London Metals Exchange (LME) or the New York Commodity Exchange (COMEX). In the *1988 World Commodity Outlook*, the Economist Intelligence Unit argued that in the aluminum industry only a smaller portion of the world consumption is traded on the LME (110,000 tons on the LME compared to 26 million tons worldwide), and that the prices of the LME are "not only unrepresentative (but) positively damaging to the industry." In 1987 LME prices were higher than producer prices, causing backwardation in the metals traded ("LME Copper Prices in Wider Backwardation," *American Metals Market*, 7 May 1985 and "Towards a Backwardation," *The Mining Journal*, 25 January 1985). But the reverse was happening in the early 1980s, in that metals prices were kept down below producer prices--due to alleged speculation in the dealer markets (cf. T. Stundza, "Metals Outlook," *Purchasing*, 7 February 1987: 66B3).

In trade articles over the years 1982-1984, it was stated that government-controlled metals producers in developing countries were a primary cause of the depressed metals prices, because they continued to produce "at high, if not record, levels" (cf. "The Year Ahead," *Mining Journal*, 7 January 1982) in the face of declining demand. The government-controlled companies followed that course either to support employment or to add to holdings of foreign currency. In the copper industry by 1982, "one third of the world copper production (was) owned by state corporations which opposed cutbacks (in production) . . . Further, 36 percent of capacity (was) owned by governments which depend on copper for the majority of their income" ("Copper: A Need for Caution," *Mining Journal*, 15 October 1982). Molybdenum, because it is a by-product of copper production, also became affected by this mis-alignment of economic objectives by governments. Nickel prices also remained depressed due to severe overcapacity, subsidization of production by governments, and excess production by Cuba and the U.S.S.R. ("Nickel: Problems Remain," *Mining Journal*, 25 March 1983).

has been argued that they have in recent years brought about successive and irreversible price declines.[4]

The first set of explanations begins on the demand side with the recognition that the metals-using industries have expanded their production in the 1980s at much lower rates than during the 1970s, so that their demands for metals have in turn expanded at lower rates.[5] At the same time, these industries have been substituting other materials for metals so as to reduce demand growth even further.[6] When growth in demand declines, inventories decline. Not only are working inventories reduced, but inventories held to hedge against future metals price increases are substantially eliminated.

Credit has been given to excessive supply growth as well as to reduced demand. Supply increased considerably in the early 1980s in part because of unrealistic expectations of producers with regard to high rates of growth of demand in metals

---

[4]Both economic and political factors are cited by the U.S. Bureau of Mines: "Overproduction by nations that rely on export of mineral commodities to support their economies and service their international debt; the strong value of the dollar relative to that of other currencies, which favors the importation of products into the U.S.; relatively high domestic labor costs compared with those of developing nations; and the use of industrial minerals such as carbon fibers, glass fibers and plastics in products historically constructed from metals, have all contributed to create chronically depressed world metals prices and markets in which the U.S. producer finds it increasingly difficult to compete" (U.S. Bureau of Mines, *1985 Minerals Yearbook* [Washington, D.C., 1985], 7).

[5]The nonferrous metals industries - copper, aluminum, molybdenum, lead, nickel, and zinc - all provide inputs to sectors of the economy, such as the construction and transportation equipment industries, that have been experiencing substantial decline. For instance, as recently as 1979 more than 40 percent of all aluminum shipments went to those industries. The effect of the limited rate of growth in those industries has probably been to reduce demands for inputs. In fact, aluminum sales dropped 35 percent and molybdenum sales dropped 15 percent in 1981 ("Still More Trimming is on the Way," *Business Week*, 11 January 1982: 94).

[6]Examples of substitutions of both materials and other metals are numerous. Columbium (niobium), manganese and vanadium replace molybdenum in certain steels (U.S. Bureau of Mines, *Molybdenum: A Chapter from Mineral Facts and Problems*, preprint [Washington, D.C., 1987], 9). Fiber optics have taken the place of copper wire in communications, while polyvinylchloride has replaced copper in many plumbing applications (T. Stundza, "Metals Outlook," *Purchasing*, 23 October 1986: 42-53). The plastic components in the U.S. passenger car increased 32.9 percent between 1976 and 1986; steel and zinc decreased 21.9 percent and 59.1 percent, respectively (*Ward's Automotive Yearbook*, 1986, 27). Pervading the nickel industry has been a diminishing degree of use: "Other materials, particularly plastics, continued to be preferred over nickel in finished products used in nonstress environments. A ubiquitous trend toward lightness and economy fostered these substitutions" (U.S. Bureau of Mines, *1985 Minerals Yearbook* [Washington, D.C., 1987], 712).

markets.[7] These mistakes increased producers' inventories, which tended to overhang the market with additional supply.

The most substantial source of supply expansion, however, has been from foreign producers expanding sales in the United States in the 1980s. These producers were mostly state-owned enterprises with large new mine projects that were initiated in the late 1970s in developing countries--projects which promised to produce at lower costs than the established older mines in the U.S. and Canada. When completed in the 1980s, they provided refined product at lower costs than expected, given that dollar exchange rates for the local currencies had increased in the intervening period. This expansion resulted in new supplies for the United States, the center of the world market, while adding to total volumes available worldwide.[8]

---

[7]High growth expectations motivated the installation of capacity. During this period, "there has been worldwide imbalance between the demand for iron and steel and production capacity. Capacity utilization in the United States, the European Economic Community and Japan in 1982 was only 57 percent; it improved only slightly in 1983 to 59 percent. This imbalance occurred because of a significant slowdown in the growth of steel demand during the 1970s. It takes a number of years to build steel plants, and projects planned or started during the steel shortage of 1973 and 1974 did not come on-stream until demand growth had turned down" (U.S. Bureau of Mines, *Iron and Steel: A Chapter from Mineral Facts and Problems*, preprint [Washington, D.C., 1985], 16).

[8] For example, in the aluminum market "in periods of declining demand, privately owned aluminum producers are disproportionately affected when subsidized government-owned smelters do not reduce output. In the recession of 1981 and 1982 producers, particularly in developing countries, but also in many European countries, maintained high [aluminum] production levels. Some government-owned companies were subsidized and continued operating at a loss. In the United States, the industry, privately owned and operated, reduced production as inventories rose and profits declined. Inventories of aluminum in most producer countries increased to twice the historical levels. Aluminum prices declined worldwide, and both integrated and independent companies sustained heavy financial losses" (U.S. Bureau of Mines, *Aluminum: A Chapter from Mineral Facts and Problems*, preprint [Washington, D.C., 1985], 17).

The most significant development to affect world copper supplies during the early 1980s has been increased production from centralized developing nationals. Increases in production in 1982 were registered by Australia, Chile, Iran, Morocco, Peru, Poland and the U.S.S.R., which together produced some 300,000 tons more than in 1981. Chile alone increased mine production in 1982 by about 160,000 tons of contained copper over the 1981 level and became the top world producer of mine copper. In that same year, copper production in the United States and Canada decreased by 25 percent and 11 percent, respectively, compared with production in 1981 (U.S. Bureau of Mines, *Copper: A Chapter from Mineral Facts and Problems*, preprint [Washington, D.C., 1985], 19).

The argument is that these changes worked through metals markets to produce new equilibrium prices. With decreased growth in metals utilization, and increased growth of mine production, market equilibrating processes then brought about the large mill-products price reductions realized in the early 1980s. That is, prices continued to fall until both production rates and the substitution of other materials had declined sufficiently to bring inventories back into balance. But under this explanation, the price reductions ceased when producers and dealers were cleared of excess inventories--there was no internal, reinforcing downward spiral in the market. Only further changes in industrial growth or dollar exchange rates would bring about further reductions in the metals price level.

The question is whether market equilibrating factors have in fact been determinative. Are the 1980-1987 price levels best described as world equilibrium prices? Indeed, quite contradictory explanations based on disequilibrating forces have been offered as providing a more complete and more accurate explanation of the general price decline.

This second set of explanations begins with focusing on the feedback to inventory-holding decisions. Reductions in general inflation rates in the early 1980s were said to have caused manufacturers to reduce their metals inventories: As prices stabilized, their prospective gains from holding stocks of metals were reduced so that their demands for metals held as inventories declined. But then metals dealers, in the face of these declines, reduced their inventories, causing demands to fall further. The feedback effect reduced total demands at lower prices.[9]

---

[9]Barry Bosworth and Robert Z. Lawrence have described two motives for holding inventories. One is the convenience yield in which "producers and consumers hold physical inventories to smooth out production, economize on transactions, and avoid the threat of an unexpected shortfall in delivery of a key input disrupting production at higher levels of fabrication." The other motive is based on speculative yields in which the commodities as assets are attractive "because of expectations about their own future prices and their usefulness in a portfolio to diversify risks of holding other assets." Evidence suggests that inventory demand explains some of the commodity price movements of the 1970s. But this finding does not distinguish between cost-reducing and speculative motives for holding inventories (B. Bosworth and R. Lawrence, *Commodity Prices and the New Inflation* [Washington, D.C.: The Brookings Institution, 1982], 79-84).

Another alleged destabilizing factor is the purposefully unprofitable behavior on the part of government-owned metals-producing companies.[10] With falling prices, their production increases as they seek to maintain their gross cash receipts.[11] While this irrationally reduces net cash receipts below those from less production[12], it is a political necessity for state-owned enterprises with fixed levels of employment that call for fixed

[10]Raymond Ball and Robert Marks in "The Economics of Government Intervention in the World Oil Market: Episodic Instability" (1986) assert that political motives affect pricing when governments are in control of production. Governments have an objective to meet a 'targeted' or budgeted level of gross revenue. "To meet specified expenditure commitments, governments respond to lower prices by pumping more oil, not less," say the authors on page 7 and they contend on page 12 that this objective predominates for government-run companies in "social" metals industry. Their table refers to direct government control:

PERCENTAGE OF PRODUCTION UNDER GOVERNMENT CONTROL

Metal	Western Production	World Production
copper	51	63
aluminum	14	34
lead	14	39
zinc	14	36
nickel	12	44

SOURCE: *Australian Financial Review*, April 9, 1985.

[11]While world copper consumption continued a downward trend that began in 1979, world refined copper inventories were increasing; in 1982, the U.S. operated at 65 percent of capacity and the rest of the world at 85 percent. In that year, "more than 60 percent of the 63 copper-producing nations of the world either increased or maintained 1981 levels of production. Significant increases were recorded for Australia, Brazil, Chile, Mongolia, Morocco, Namibia, Peru, Poland and the U.S.S.R." (U.S. Bureau of Mines, *1982 Minerals Yearbook*, 271). Though Australia's and Brazil's copper industries are privately owned, those of the other countries have been mostly owned by the respective governments. For instance, Chile's government-owned CODELCO produced 83 percent of Chilean copper in 1982. In Peru, the state-owned companies MINERO PERU and CENTROMIN PERU (with the privately owned SPCC) accounted for 81 percent of mine production. The Intergovernmental Council of Copper Exporting Countries (CIPEC) continued to support high production levels despite the downward trend in consumption and prices (ibid., 280).

[12]With limits on mine capacity, marginal costs of production increase with output. Whatever the previous rate of output, net operating income cannot be increased by expanding production when prices fall. This is because marginal costs exceed price for that additional output.

monthly wage bills.[13] To the extent that the public-sector companies follow such procedures, they add to supply in periods of falling prices.[14]

Together, these two alleged determinants bring about conditions of lesser demand and greater supply at lower prices. Such conditions at the same time cause prices to continue to fall once they begin a downward movement.[15] Contrary to the results of an equilibrium process, they cannot be said to bring about a stable price level.[16]

What actually has happened? The most direct answer can be found in the way in which supply changed when prices

---

[13]Because the metal-producing industries are seen as important sources of employment, the "response of reducing production in cases of losses caused by low prices is a politically less viable option" for government-owned enterprises (Thomas Walde, "World Mineral Development: Current Issues," *Columbia Journal of World Business*, Vol. 19 #1 [Spring 1984]: 28).

[14]"As copper prices have dropped [in 1983], mines in the Third World countries have increased their output to make up for lost revenues. This has created a severe supply-demand imbalance pushing the copper price 'below the [production cost] breakeven point for the best U.S. mines,' says George Cleaver, an industry analyst at Merrill Lynch Pierce Fenner & Smith, Inc." ("Aluminum Surges as Other Metals also Rise," *Business Week*, 21 March 1984, 252).

[15]Ball and Marks (1986) contend that when government-controlled companies have a 'revenue target', and "if an exogenous contraction in demand occurs, then at least some producers initially find themselves on the 'long' side of the market, with excess supply. They thus are unable to meet their revenue targets . . . Competition among suppliers for scarce buyers results in downward pressure on price, which exacerbates the excess supply in the market. . . Thus the price is unstable in a downward direction, at least in the short run" (ibid., 7).

[16]Speculation and hedging in commodities markets are cited for increasing prices further when prices are rising. Richard N. Cooper and Robert Z. Lawrence have explored the rise in commodity prices during the 1972-1974 period of worldwide economic expansion. They have found that the rapid growth in demand for consumption uses accounts for a sizable portion of the rise in commodity prices and that a "seeming shortage" of supply did not explain much at all. However, they conclude that the "'unexplained' part of the price movements can be reasonably attributed to 'speculative' hedging demand for commodities." Several measures are provided for increased "speculation". Though it is impossible to "differentiate between pure speculation and hedging by users, the demand for long forward positions in commodities grew substantially (and were) accompanied by sharp increases in both price and volume at the end of 1973 and early 1974." Contributing factors in the increase in evident speculation or hedging activities were worldwide inflation, exchange-rate volatility and price controls. For example, with respect to exchange-rate volatility, "for a country, such as Japan, going long on internationally traded commodities needed for future production was a way to reduce large dollar holdings of uncertain value." Thus, Cooper and Lawrence identify the volatility in commodity prices as a function of the increased speculation and hedging activity (R. Cooper and R. Lawrence, "The 1972-75 Commodity Boom," *Brookings Papers on Economic Activity*, 3 [1975]: 672, 702, 704).

began to decline.[17] As has been shown, there has been a one-sixth to two-thirds drop in the prices of molybdenum, lead and copper since 1980. But while the production or supply of molybdenum has decreased appreciably, that of lead has stayed roughly the same, and that of copper has increased (see Table One). While producer prices of both steel and zinc have increased by close to 20 percent, production or supply has declined for steel and increased for zinc.

No clear pattern in keeping with one explanation or the other emerges from the aggregative movements of prices and supply. Neither declines, as expected from demand-driven but equilibrating market forces; neither consistently moves in the opposite direction. To support the disequilibrating theory, prices and quantities would have to move by increasing amounts in the opposite direction, as in a frenzy of either negative or positive speculative behavior.

A more complex analysis is required. In order to validate one of the alternative explanations, price equations are developed here to estimate the importance of each potential explanatory factor. The first equation incorporates determinants of price levels, while the second focuses on changes in prices.

The price level equation indicates the equilibrating effects of demand and supply changes or, alternatively, shows the results of disequilibrating speculation on public-company expansion. One or the other explanation is validated by the signs of the coefficients of the determining factors in the equation.

The price change equation shows directly the existence of destabilizing elements. That there are significant coefficients for the determining variables of an equation for the change in prices is an indication that metals markets have been in a price spiral. Speculation and supply surges have taken over metals markets.

Each equation is fitted on two data sets--one for dealer prices and the other for producer prices--where each set contains observations on three to as many as seven metals. The method for fitting is "generalized differencing" of each variable and then using least-squares regression (for the purpose of removing bias

---

[17] Production and supply are assumed to remain the same, or to change by the same amount. This is equivalent to being in equilibrium with respect to the current level of inventory in each year.

Table One. Metals and Industrial Production

Year	*Aluminum*	*Copper*	*Lead*	*Molybdenum*	*Nickel*	*Steel*	*Zinc*	*World Industrial Production*
				1980 = 100				
1975	77.32	88.11	83.50	73.35	111.10	91.06	83.38	81.40
1976	79.65	93.44	93.03	81.84	111.30	97.41	91.67	88.50
1977	88.11	96.73	98.76	88.14	113.10	94.74	94.73	92.10
1978	90.33	98.17	99.82	90.99	83.22	100.00	95.33	95.70
1979	92.70	99.93	100.88	94.75	87.46	106.37	104.66	100.40
1980	100.00	100.00	100.00	100.00	100.00	100.00	100.00	100.00
1981	97.53	103.53	97.17	98.19	90.36	99.04	101.67	100.10
1982	84.25	100.58	94.68	89.11	80.16	85.63	96.74	97.60
1983	86.89	103.26	94.70	49.19	83.81	87.41	103.91	100.60
1984	99.95	101.75	94.88	82.96	92.69	95.76	108.71	104.90
1985	95.82	99.78	96.19	85.75	98.17	96.34	111.46	106.30
1986	94.35	105.24	96.90	75.82	87.64	93.00	108.86	108.10

SOURCES: Industrial production, United Nations, *Monthly Bulletin of Statistics* (various issues, 1960-1988); metals production for aluminum, copper, lead and zinc, American Bureau of Metal Statistics, Inc., *Non-Ferrous Metal Data* (various issues, 1960-1987); for molybdenum, nickel and steel, U.S. Bureau of Mines, *Minerals Yearbook* (various issues, 1960-1985), and U.S. Bureau of Mines *Mineral Commodity Summaries*, (1984-1988).

from testing for the significance of the coefficients of each variable, as explained in Appendix B). Within the fitted price equation, the estimated coefficient of each independent variable provides a test for the significance of the variable as an explanatory factor. The coefficients' being positive or negative serves as the basis for assessing whether the 1980s price reductions were "explained" better by either equilibrating or disequilibrating forces. The equations are then used to project 1990s metals prices, based on the presumption that those determinants that are today significant will continue to dominate markets in the decade to come.

What are Prices?

Before finding determinants of price levels, it must be stated what "prices" are. There are extremely large numbers of transactions in metals each day--at mine, mill and delivery points. Sales involve ore, refined product and metal compounds. However, only some of these sales indicate the terms and conditions that clear unwarranted inventory accumulation or decumulation. In most instances, prices with these characteristics have been "dealer" prices and/or "producer" prices for refined product at a stated location. Dealer transactions, which have grown in volume in recent years, call for current delivery of a fixed amount at a specified price. Producer transactions provide current and future delivery of unspecified amounts at a currently specified price. During the first five years of the 1980s, as both of these prices declined dealer prices were lower than producer prices (see Table Two).[18] The dealer market has grown as dealer prices have further decreased, which suggests that producer prices have become less the means for market clearing.

---

[18]This is not a unique pattern. According to David L. McNicol (1975) producer prices were lower than dealer prices in the 1970s for copper. But this does not appear to have been the case for other metals for which both prices have been available for long periods in the 1960s and 1970s. The explanation lies in the expected relationship between current dealer prices and future producer prices.

Even so, both dealer and producer transactions play important roles in metals markets.[19] Dealer prices eliminate deficient or excess inventories from day to day, for those holding inventory speculatively or for others meeting final-goods production schedules. For industrial buyers, producer prices determine the costs of metals utilization in goods production over months or years.[20] Moreover, linkage between the two price systems can be established by shifts of demand from one type of transaction to the other. Industrial buyers increase demand in the current dealer market to add to inventory when prices in that market are below the present discounted value of expected future producer prices. Their purchases increase current dealer prices until the present value differential is eliminated. Conversely, dealers sell short and cover by buying from producers if current dealer prices are higher than the estimate of the present value of future producer prices.[21] Dealer purchases later cause producer prices to rise, restoring the present value equality of all prices.

Disparities between dealer and producer prices do arise, however, when expected producer prices are not realized. If demands are lower than expected, current dealer prices fall below current producer prices--and attempts are made by buyers to reduce their contract receipts until producer prices fall. The equilibrating process continues as demand shifts to the dealer market. This system should work so that expected prices in fact

---

[19]Approximately 50 to 70 percent of the world's nickel production is sold under long-term contracts by producers but based on LME dealer prices. As nickel prices tripled on the LME during March 1988, "producers viewed the current LME level as accurately reflecting a nickel shortage, even though in the past some of these producers had been at pains to demonstrate that LME prices were faulty indicators of real market conditions" ("Nickel Crisis Spurs Call for Fixed Pricing," *American Metals Market*, 16 March 1988).

[20]These prices are found in producer agreements, but are also characteristic of shipments in which a producer rather than a commodities broker delivers without fixed limits. In this book, the average annual London or New York Metals Exchange prices have been used to represent dealer prices; the average annual contract price from trade publications represents producer prices.

[21]Uncertainty has its effects as well. There should be a premium in producer over dealer prices by an amount necessary to compensate producers for fixed prices. Otherwise, sales would shift in large volume to future contracts, given their relative security, until prices in those transactions increased relative to producer or spot transactions.

systematically do not develop disparities over long periods.[22] While prices move apart because of current events, the linkage should be direct over a 15-year period as market participants correct, and learn from, their forecast errors.

Both dealer and producer prices are used to represent systematic market behavior. The price series are for United States delivery, as quoted on major dealer exchanges and by expert agents seeking market-clearing producer prices. Dealer prices respond in equilibrium to changing demands or in disequilibrium to speculative behavior, and more sensitively than producer prices, given relatively fixed dealer supply in current exchange markets. Spot or dealer prices are analyzed for four metals for which there was continuous dealer trading over the 1970-1987 period. Contract or producer prices constitute the terms at which purchases and sales are equalized over longer periods and thus determine the scale of the supply side of all metals markets. Producer prices for seven metals--carbon steel, copper, aluminum, molybdenum, nickel, lead, and zinc--are analyzed for the 1960-1987 period.

Specifying Price Determinants in an Equilibration Process

Producer prices for metals decreased in the early 1980s at the same time that industrial production and general wholesale prices increased. Dealer prices fell even more than producer prices (as in Table Two). As has been stated, this departure of metals from other prices cannot be explained--at least not by a macroscopic analysis of concurrent price and supply changes in the seven metals. A more exacting and complete analysis begins

---

[22]Assume that expected prices are realized over long periods of time, or that forecast errors are random with zero mean. Then consider the equation $P_c = a + bP_s$ where P_c is producer and P_s is dealer price. For prices to move together, "a" should be zero and "b" should be 1.0. Copper for the period 1971-1985 is an example:

$$P_c = -0.132 + 0.893P_s$$

with the "a" value of -0.132 being insignificantly different from zero, and the "b" value of 0.893 being insignificantly different from 1.0. The same equation fitted to data for this period for aluminum, lead and zinc resulted in "b" coefficients not significantly different from 1.0 in each case. The sources for data used in this regression are noted in Table Three.

Table Two. Dealer and Producer Prices

Year	Aluminum		Copper		Lead		Molybdenum		Nickel		Steel	Zinc	
	(D)	*(P)*	*(D)*	*(P)*	*(D)*	*(P)*	*(D)*	*(P)*	*(D)*	*(P)*	*(P)*	*(D)*	*(P)*
					(Dollars per pound)								
1975	0.31	0.40	0.56	0.65	0.19	0.22	2.82	2.62	1.89	2.07	0.13	0.34	0.39
1976	0.39	0.45	0.64	0.70	0.20	0.23	3.73	3.15	2.08	2.25	0.13	0.32	0.38
1977	0.45	0.51	0.60	0.67	0.28	0.31	5.35	4.01	2.08	2.41	0.15	0.27	0.34
1978	0.48	0.54	0.62	0.72	0.30	0.34	9.88	4.95	1.93	2.05	0.17	0.27	0.31
1979	0.69	0.61	0.90	0.92	0.55	0.53	25.33	7.50	2.56	2.75	0.18	0.34	0.39
1980	0.79	0.71	0.99	1.02	0.41	0.43	9.63	9.70	3.08	3.41	0.21	0.35	0.38
1981	0.61	0.77	0.79	0.86	0.33	0.37	6.62	8.50	2.87	3.43	0.23	0.38	0.45
1982	0.47	0.76	0.67	0.75	0.25	0.26	4.20	4.00	2.33	3.20	0.25	0.34	0.40
1983	0.68	0.78	0.72	0.78	0.19	0.22	3.60	3.64	2.18	3.20	0.26	0.35	0.43
1984	0.61	0.81	0.63	0.69	0.20	0.27	3.45	3.56	2.21	3.20	0.27	0.42	0.50
1985	0.49	0.81	0.63	0.69	0.19	0.20	3.35	3.33	2.22	2.01	0.28	0.33	0.42
1986	0.56	0.81	0.63	0.68	0.19	0.22	3.14	3.10	1.84	3.20	0.25	0.35	0.41
1987	0.71	0.88	0.78	0.80	0.26	0.36	2.96	3.25	2.19	5.15	0.25	0.37	0.44

D = Dealer, P = Producer

SOURCES: Dealer prices, International Bank for Reconstruction and Development (IBRD), *Commodity Trade and Price Trends* (1985), U.S. Bureau of Mines, *Mineral Commodity Summaries, 1987,* and *Metals Week* (various issues). Producer prices for aluminum, copper, lead and zinc, Standard and Poor's Corporation, *Basic Statistics on Metals, 1984,* and U.S. Bureau of Mines, *Mineral Commodity Summaries, 1984-1985,* for molybdenum and nickel, Amax Corporation; for steel, International Bank for Reconstruction and Development, *Commodity Trade and Price Trends* (1986).

with specifying four independent variables that affect price levels: two in demand and two in supply. These variables work by affecting price levels until excess or deficient inventories are eliminated.

Demand Factors. The demands for metals are either for direct use or for inventory accumulation. In the most general terms, the volume of metal for use in production is determined by the revenue to be gained from additional sales of those final products, by prices of that metal, and by competing and complementary inputs in final products. But, given that such revenue productivity cannot be observed, the determinants of demands are metals prices, final goods prices, and the level of constant dollar final goods production.[23]

Demands for metals inventories behave differently from those for metals to be used in production. Buyers hold stocks to reduce the costs associated with interrupted production, and they accumulate such stocks until additional holding costs exceed the potential savings from more production smoothing. When prices fall, accumulation increases because holding costs decrease; accumulation increases with the general price index since higher prices make future production smoothing costs greater. Thus demand for inventories should increase when metals prices decrease or other prices increase. In order to account for both effects, the metals and industrial price indices are treated as independent determinants of the inventory demand for metals.[24]

Producer and dealer price differentials also affect the demands for inventory. Inventory accumulation continues until the present value of expected producer and dealer prices are the same, so that it is increased by reductions in current dealer price levels or by increases in expected inflation rates. That is, lower current metals prices and higher inflation rates open up profit

---

[23]Total product is a surrogate for marginal product in that year-to-year changes in total product, with stable technology and expected changes in metals utilization, provide time-related estimates of marginal product.

[24]The demand relationship is affected by the price of metals substitutes. But the general industrial price level can be expected to correlate with the price of substitutes when substitutes include a wide range of industrial products. Then the industrial price level, when it reflects the costs of a wide range of inputs to the manufacturing process, can be treated as a surrogate for the price of substitutes.

opportunities gained from accumulating inventory, and current demands are thereby increased.

Taking account of both utilization and inventory determinants, the demands for metals at time t can be specified as:

$$D_t = Q_{d,t} + S_t \qquad (1)$$

for production use $Q_{d,t}$ and inventory accumulation S_t. Then the demands of final users for new volumes of metal not in inventory can be stated as:

$$Q_{d,t} = f(IQ_t, P_t, S_{t-1}, GPL_t) \qquad (2)$$

The process of market equilibration determines the positive or negative signs for the coefficients of the right-hand-side variables in this relationship. Demands increase with industrial production (IQ_t) and with the general price level (GPL_t) in major consuming countries.[25] Demands are reduced by larger stocks at the start of the period (S_{t-1}) because holding costs are higher. Demands are reduced as the current metals price (P_t) climbs higher.

Supply factors. The determinants of metals supply are prices measured against the marginal costs of current mine and mill production. The marginal costs depend in turn on input prices such as wage rates, and on mine and mill capacity. Supply comes from both production and inventories, and the marginal costs of using the existing inventories in the system depend on the level of such stocks and interest rates. But over longer periods, capacity and inventory constraints are not as critical because producers add to capacity by developing existing or newly discovered reserves. This process for bringing new sources into production, while quite complex, is basically justified by reductions in marginal costs to levels lower than those for further output from reserves already being exploited. Yet, given current

---

[25] As has already been mentioned, the general price level variable serves as a surrogate for the price of substitutes as well as a measure of inflation. Higher values of GPL_t should add to demands, because of higher metal revenue product; they should increase demands for inventory, for the reason cited in the preceding paragraph.

factor costs, capacity and inventories, production is pushed to the level at which marginal costs of production or stock depletion equal the marginal revenues received on sale. Under competitive or noncompetitive conditions, the supply function is as follows:[26]

$$Q_{S,t} = f(P_t, K_t, S_t). \qquad (3)$$

Metals supply $Q_{S,t}$ in year t is positively related to the price P_t of that commodity, the level of capacity K_t and the level of producer-held inventories or stocks S_t. When non-competitive conditions prevail, as with nickel or molybdenum at certain times, then the producer price is set first and supply is then held at levels necessary to clear markets of current demands. That is,

$$P_t = f(K_t, S_t, Q_{P,t}). \qquad (4)$$

Another potentially important supply determinant is the dollar exchange rate for foreign currencies. Since the geographic center of the trade in most metals is the United States, and because prices are in U.S. dollars, dollar appreciation has the effect of reducing foreign costs of production relative to foreign receipts from dollar-sales prices. For those depreciated-currency supply sources that receive dollars for sales, the profit margins on metals production increase--which of course causes those countries to increase their supply.[27] To take account of these effects, which result from relative factor to output price declines, the supply function incorporates a determining variable (XI_t) for the index value of the dollar, weighted by country exports to the U.S. for each metal. As XI_t increases, then supplies from foreign sources should increase.

---

[26]Factor prices are accounted for in the general price index.

[27]"... steel mills in the developing countries have become the world's lowest cost producers, with their lower costs partly the result of weakened currencies versus the dollar, 'spot' market purchases of raw materials, and managerial efforts at cost reduction. The newly 'steel-active' countries, such as Argentina, Mexico, Brazil, Venezuela, South Africa, Taiwan and South Korea, have taken an expanding portion of the export market. Whereas seven of these countries were net importers of 13 million short tons of steel in 1974, by 1985 the same countries were net exporters of 15 million tons" (U.S. International Trade Commission, "Annual Survey Concerning Competitive Conditions in the Steel Industry and Efforts to Adjust and Modernize", USITC Publication 1881 [September 1986], 38).

Derivation of the "Supply/Demand" Price Equation. As a result of the equilibrium process, metals prices are determined by industrial production, the general price level, the volume of stocks, and the exchange rate.[28] Equating quantities demanded $Q_{d,t}$ and supplied $Q_{s,t}$ in equations (2) and (3), so as to replicate the process of market clearing of excess or deficient inventories, results in a price level equation with four determining variables:

$$P_t = f(IQ_t, S_{t-1}, GPL_t, XI_t) \qquad (5)$$

The relationships between prices and these variables are critical to a market-clearing equilibrium. The greater the industrial production and inflation, the higher the prices should be. And the greater the beginning-of-the-year stocks and the higher the exchange rate for the dollar, the lower the prices should be. Thus the signs of the price relationships for IQ_t and GPL_t should be positive--while S_{t-1} and XI_t should be negative--if the process of market clearing is to work.

To the extent that this equation describes actual producer and dealer prices, then these determinants and an equilibrium process can be said to explain both the 1970s price behavior and the 1980s price collapse.[29] More specifically, if recent years prices are close to those expected from fitting this price equation to the entire time-series of such prices, then these four determinants can be said to have operated to clear markets.

---

[28] Measures of capacity are not available to the extent that analysis at this level of aggregation can be supported. Further work is underway, however, to extend this research in a direction that will allow for direct measures of coefficients of capacity.

[29] Bosworth and Lawrence hypothesize that the commodity prices in the mid-70s were a "result of a synchronized and excessive growth of aggregate demand in the principal consuming nations and did not constitute a special problem in and of themselves." A supplementary hypothesis is that "the rise in relative prices (is) evidence of a long-term trend toward exhaustion of natural resources" (cf. B. Bosworth and R. Lawrence, *Commodity Prices and the New Inflation*, 62). While they do not support this hypothesis with their own argument, they do test relative nonferrous metals prices in the context of a reduced form price equation in which both demand and supply determinants are present (see Table 4-3, results of equations for relative prices of nonferrous metals, ibid., 76).

Disequilibrium Price Behavior

The alternative explanation is that the metals markets became unstable in the mid-1980s in response to a sharp initial round of reductions in 1980-1981. Prices fell first in response to reduced rates of growth of metals usage in world goods production, and when it later became evident to inventory holders that inflation rates were on the decline, inventory-holders' demands decline. But that round of reductions itself caused a more serious collapse.

There are two plausible unstable sequences--the first on the producer side and the other on the buyer side of metals markets. The supply side argument is that certain sources generate a production strategy that causes total market supply to decrease with price. These sources consist of public enterprises in developing countries that open new mines and expand milling capacity to obtain cash flow to pay wages for large numbers of unskilled workers. With employment an end in itself for such enterprises (see Funkhauser and MacAvoy 1979), an initial round of reduced prices causes the developing countries to increase their production to meet their politically-determined wage bills (see Adelman 1986; Ball and Marks 1986). If these public enterprises constitute the marginal sources in the world market, then initial price reductions would generate increased market-wide supply--and further price reductions would be brought forth.[30]

The demand-side argument is that inventories are determined by dealers' speculation on future price levels. The fabricators' and dealers' holdings of stocks fall as prices fall, given that their expectation is that future prices will be lower as indicated by these initial price reductions. This sequence reverses the direction of processes associated with market

---

[30]Metal by-products seemingly affect supply growth in ways that are different from normal supply-demand economics. For instance, in 1985 when world production of lead exceeded demand, an 80,000-ton increase of additional mine capacity occurred. This was mostly due to new zinc and/or silver operations. Similarly molybdenum production increased by 9 percent at the Chuquicamata mine of CODELCO (the largest copper mine in the world) in 1982 at a time when global mine molybdenum production exceeded demand. The molybdenum increase was due to Chile's increased copper production (U.S. Bureau of Mines, *1985 Minerals Yearbook*, 604, 708).

clearing, in that price decreases cause reductions in the quantity demanded.

How can we determine whether these political and expectational factors have been the cause of the price collapse, rather than the previously posited four market equilibration factors? To the extent that such government expansion of Third World production capacity--and dealer inventory speculation--played dominant roles, then world markets would have been characterized by demand below supply following a significant initial price reduction. The price level equation 5 would follow a disequilibrating process by which the signs of the relationships would be reversed. That is, the lower the inventories and the exchange rate for the dollar, the greater would be the prices. And the greater the industrial production and inflation rates, the lower would be the prices. In the presence of destabilizing conditions, the signs of the price relationships with all the independent variables would be the reverse of those when equilibrium conditions prevail.[31]

There is a second indirect test for the presence of disequilibrating behavior. The signs of the coefficients in the price level equation provide a direct test. Another, dynamic equation examines the process of price change itself. If disequilibrium conditions prevail, any price change only increases the gap between demand and supply. As has already been argued, a sharp price decrease would be followed by more supply in excess of less demand. Prices subsequent to the initial change would change in the same direction and by a greater amount. In equation 6, with this period's price change P_t dependent on that last period P_{t-1},

$$\Delta P_t = a + b\Delta P_{t-1} \qquad (6)$$

[31]Consider the supply function in equation 3 and the demand function in equation 2 to be both linear equations, and assume that at the time of observation supply and demand prices are the same. Then the coefficients of the independent variables in the price level equation 5 have in their denominators the coefficients of supply price minus demand price. If the coefficient of supply price is negative, and that of demand price is positive, as in this disequilibrating argument, then the denominator is negative. This implies that the coefficients of production and inflation will be negative and those of stocks and exchange rates positive.

the constant term "a" would be zero and the coefficient "b" would be greater than 1.0 because of this expansive process.

If such disequilibrating forces took over the price formation process in the middle 1980s, then equation 6 should describe year-to-year changes in that period. Metals markets can be said to have been characterized by implosive "bubbles", given that one of two steps took place. What is most basic is that the last two decades of price behavior should have been dominated by price changes that fit the equation 6 pattern. But what is more specific to recent events is that the actual changes after 1980 have been dominated by previous changes rather than by factors that are part of the equilibration process.

Chapter Two describes the price level and price change equations fitted to data on seven metals for the 1960-1987 period. The chapter also contains tests for the explanatory value of the equilibration process over the "bubble" argument for recent behavior.

Chapter Two

EXPLANATORY PRICE EQUATIONS

In the 1970s and 1980s, the diversification of metals-producing companies across countries and products created a single market. For the most part, metals prices moved together in response to economy-wide forces. While the level of copper prices differed from that of aluminum, because of differences by grade in mining and milling costs, year-to-year changes in the two sets of prices moved together. When copper demand increased (while aluminum did not), copper prices rose relative to aluminum; this caused, however, a shift of resources by the diversified metals-producing companies from aluminum to copper supply until the original price differentials were restored. Such convergence of year-to-year changes in prices of one or the other metal has taken place in a general way in the last twenty years. A sufficient number of producers have operated across the different metals to expand supply where specific ore prices were relatively high and to reduce supply where prices were low relative to the overall metals price index.[32]

---

[32]Indicative of the effects of supply in separate metals is the correlation of producer and dealer prices across metals. Low copper prices are accompanied by low aluminum prices to the extent that simple correlation coefficients of copper-aluminum price pairs in the 1960-1986 time period was 0.791. This correlation would have occurred by chance in a distribution of all pairs of prices. The simple correlation coefficients of the seven metals are similarly high, as shown in the two tables on the following page.

There have been significant exceptions. Molybdenum and nickel prices have diverged in year-to-year changes from the others, because reserve holdings of these two metals have in each case been dominated by a single company, making expansion or

---

PRICE CORRELATIONS: PRODUCER PRICES

Metal	Aluminum	Copper	Lead	Zinc	Nickel	Molyb-denum	Steel
Aluminum	1.00000 0.0000	0.79055 0.0001	0.68679 0.0001	0.91110 0.0001	0.92623 0.0001	0.68288 0.0001	0.98937 0.0001
Copper	0.79055 0.0001	1.00000 0.0000	0.87738 0.0001	0.87299 0.0001	0.90410 0.0001	0.82880 0.0001	0.79869 0.0001
Lead	0.68679 0.0001	0.87738 0.0001	1.00000 0.0000	0.73427 0.0001	0.78937 0.0001	0.91940 0.0001	0.65705 0.0002
Zinc	0.91110 0.0001	0.87299 0.0001	0.73427 0.0001	1.00000 0.0000	0.93241 0.0001	0.65861 0.0002	0.93078 0.0001
Nickel	0.92623 0.0001	0.90410 0.0001	0.78937 0.0001	0.93241 0.0001	1.00000 0.0000	0.77170 0.0001	0.91512 0.0001
Molyb-denum	0.68288 0.0001	0.82880 0.0001	0.91940 0.0001	0.65861 0.0002	0.77170 0.0001	1.00000 0.0000	0.63057 0.0004
Steel	0.98937 0.0001	0.79869 0.0001	0.65705 0.0002	0.93078 0.0001	0.91512 0.0001	0.63057 0.0004	1.00000 0.0000

PRICE CORRELATIONS: DEALER PRICES

Metal	Aluminum	Copper	Lead	Zinc
Aluminum	1.00000 0.0000	0.69817 0.0001	0.81813 0.0001	0.75277 0.0001
Copper	0.69817 0.0001	1.00000 0.0000	0.76821 0.0001	0.74387 0.0001
Lead	0.81813 0.0001	0.76821 0.0001	1.00000 0.0000	0.65895 0.0002
Zinc	0.75277 0.0001	0.74387 0.0001	0.65895 0.0002	1.00000 0.0000

The probability of occurrence, shown below the correlation coefficient, is sufficiently small as to reject the hypothesis that the two prices are correlated by chance in this sample.

contraction of these metals relatively difficult.[33] But the presumption is that metals prices move together in responses to significant changes in metals inventories and producing capacity, or to cyclical or inflationary shocks in the world economy.

To determine the source of the metals price collapse of the 1980s then requires an appraisal of an "index" of prices. This index is formulated here by pooling the separate metals price series, and thereby constructing a single data set. In the price level equations, copper price is the constant term; the other metals prices adjust to their separate levels by the addition of dummy (0,1) variables.

The Price Level Equation

The impact of various price determinants is indicated in equations fitted to the pooled data from the seven separate metals. The observations of both dealer and producer prices and of the determining variables are for the years 1960-1986.[34]

---

[33]Prior to 1982 the U.S. provided over 50 percent of the non-communist world's molybdenum supply, most of which originated at primary mines owned by Amax Corporation. "The country's three primary molybdenum mines (Climax, Henderson and Questa) provided about 70 percent of the total U.S. output in 1980. . . Amax's Climax and Henderson mines, the two major molybdenum mines of the world, together produced over 102 million pounds of molybdenum in 1980. This quantity represented about 68 percent of U.S. output and 43 percent of total world output" (U.S. Bureau of Mines, *1980 Minerals Yearbook*, 574).

Also, before the 1970s the International Nickel Corporation (INCO) dominated the nickel market and effectively determined nickel prices (or tags). But, "INCO has fallen . . . from the days when it was 'The Nickel Company,' with 90 percent of the free world's production of a mineral (nickel)" (Peter Brimelow, "No Nickel Plugged," *Barron's*, 7 December 1981). Since 1980 . . . "major producers, INCO and Falconbridge in North America and Le Nickel in France, no longer dictate tags. The pricing barometer today is the London Metals Exchange price" (T. Stundza, "Metals Outlook," *Purchasing*, 12 February 1987, 66B9).

[34]The data for the determining variables were obtained from sources as follows:

INDUSTRIAL PRODUCTION. The world industrial production data series was collected from issues of *Monthly Bulletin of Statistics*, United Nations. "World" industrial production consists of production in the non-communist world only. In many instances, index numbers have been computed from official statistics provided by countries.

METAL STOCKS. The metal stock data includes both producer and consumer inventories. They were compiled by Chase Econometrics for Amax Corporation. An index with 1980 as the

Observations are available for dealer prices for only four of the metals; for producer prices there are observations for all seven metals.

The constant terms for price levels have been estimated as shown in Table Three. Treating the level of dealer or spot copper price as the basic term, adjustment terms to the constant labeled D1 to D3 have been estimated for dealer or spot prices of aluminum, lead and zinc, for which there are continuous time series. Similarly, with the producer or contract price of copper as the constant, adjustment terms labeled D1 to D6 have been estimated for the level of producer or contract prices for each of the remaining six metals. This follows the convergent process by which price changes of the seven metals tend to equalize.

The dealer price level equation indicates that changes in industrial production, the price index, inventories, and the exchange rate have been significant joint determinants of actual prices of four metals.[35] The coefficient for industrial production is positive and significantly different from zero; that for the general price index is positive but not significantly different from zero. The coefficient for stocks is negative and significant, as is that for the exchange rate index. Sixty-nine percent of the year-to-year variations in prices are explained by the equation, as indicated by a value for the calculated R-square of 0.689.

Similar results have been obtained from fitting the price level equation to pooled producer or contract prices for all seven

---

base year has been constructed from the Amax data. Metal inventory for steel is for the United States only.

WHOLESALE PRICE INDEX. The wholesale price index has been compiled from "The International Financial Statistics Yearbook," published by the International Monetary Fund. World indices are compiled by taking weighted averages of the country indexes, using real GNP as weights.

PRODUCER EXCHANGE RATE. The producer exchange rate variable used in the regression is an index with 1980 as the base year. The exchange rate is the weighted average exchange rate for the five largest metals-producing countries. Exchange rates for these five countries in national currency units per U.S. dollar are indexed with 1980 as the base year. The indexed exchange rate for the country is then multiplied by the metal production for that country. The resultant product term is used to compile weighted average.

[35]The regression equation is significant in explaining this pooled price series. The regression as a whole "fits" the data, as concluded from the "significant" value of the F statistic. Pindyck and Rubinfeld (1981) provide a detailed discussion of this position.

Table Three. Price Equations for 1960-1986

Independent Variables	*Dealer Prices* (*Dollars per pound*)	*Producer Prices*
Intercept	-0.2126 (-0.564)	0.3448 (1.928) *
World Industrial Production	1.1956 (3.882) *	0.3107 (1.628)
Metal Stocks	-0.1716 (-2.721) *	-0.0592 (-1.538)
Wholesale Price Index	0.0508 (0.374)	0.4780 (5.649) *
Exchange Rate Index	-0.6455 (-2.275) *	-0.3107 (3.412) *
D1 Aluminum	-0.4569 -(3.460) *	-0.3294 (-2.812) *
D2 Lead	-1.2446 (-10.024) *	-1.1360 (-9.868) *
D3 Zinc	-0.9412 (-8.695) *	-0.7956 (8.417) *
D4 Steel	N/A	-1.5841 (-14.887) *
D5 Nickel	N/A	1.1513 (9.254) *
D6 Molybdenum	N/A	1.6022 (13.680) *
R-Square	0.6893	0.9131
F-Statistic	30.112 (7,95)	187.09 (10,167)
Durbin-Watson	1.588	1.544

SOURCES: Dealer prices, *Metals Week* (various issues), and IBRD, *Commodity Trade and Price Trends* (1986); Producer prices for aluminum, copper, lead and zinc, Standard and Poor's Corporation, *Basic Statistics on Metals, 1984*, and U.S. Bureau of Mines, *Mineral Commodity Summaries 1988*, for molybdenum and nickel, Amax Corporation.

NOTE: All variables are in logarithms, and the equation is estimated by generalized differencing. The t-statistic for each coefficient is shown below the coefficient in parenthesis (see Pindyck and Rubinfeld 1981). For an explanation on how to calculate the individual generalized differenced variables, see Appendix B.

* statistically significant

metals.[36] These prices, similar to dealer prices, have been determined by industrial production levels, stock changes, inflation rates, and the dollar exchange rate. The coefficient for industrial production, though positive, is not significant; it can only be concluded that increases in general economic activity had a marginal impact on current dollar prices set by producers in continuing contracts for these metals. But the coefficient for the inflation rate index is positive and significant, which is consistent with the expectation that inflation has caused contract prices of metals to increase, if not in a one-to-one relationship.[37] The coefficient for stock levels is negative and significant for the pooled producer or contract price series, so that an increase in stocks substantially reduced nominal producer metals prices in contract deliveries over time. Changes in dollar exchange rates had the expected impact, given that the coefficient of the exchange rate is negative and significantly different from zero. Three of the four variables had significant price impacts, and the equation explained close to 91 percent of the variation in the seven metals producer prices.[38]

Both dealer and producer prices were associated, as expected from the operation of market equilibrating forces, with the level of stocks and the rate of inflation. Reductions in stocks, and increases in general inflation, caused metals prices to

---

[36]These are prices set by producers at levels they believe to be sustainable, given their forecasts of demands for the next year or more. Fisher, Cootner, Baily (1972), Hubbard (1986), and MacKinnon and Olewiler (1980) have analyzed this price system in both the copper and oil markets. Hubbard suggests that dealer prices are essentially short-term prices, with producer prices being long-run prices. Verleger (1982) concludes that it is the dealer market that drives the oil pricing system, since the dealer price is the marginal price. Bohi (1983) and Hubbard disprove Verleger's conclusions, based on empirical findings. Hubbard concludes that the appropriate marginal price is not the dealer price but a weighted average of the dealer price and the price at which new contracts are signed.

[37]The percentage increase in metals prices is 0.644 of the percentage increase in the inflation index. A high degree of correlation exists between the two demand variables, which at least partly explains the lack of one-to-one variation with the industrial production coefficient (cf. Pindyck and Rubinfeld 1981; Harnett 1982).

[38]Given that the value of R-square is 0.913, the null hypothesis that the coefficients for the independent variables jointly have zero explanatory power can be safely rejected for all the metals, given that the F-statistic is significant (cf. Pindyck and Rubinfeld 1981).

rise during the 1960-1986 period.[39] Much the same can be concluded with respect to the variation of metals prices as they relate to industrial production and exchange rates. As industrial production increased, metals prices rose (but did so significantly only for dealer prices and not for producer prices). As exchange rates for the dollar increased, both dealer and producer prices fell significantly.[40] And the price level equation containing the four determinants explained a large percentage of the price variance--more than 69 percent for dealer prices and 91 percent for producer prices.

If markets had been dominated throughout this period by inventory speculation, and by the politically determined additions to supply of the government mining companies in the developing countries, then the signs of all these determining variables would have been reversed. The coefficients of industrial production and inflation would have been negative, and those for stocks and exchange rates positive, if disequilibrating processes had dominated the 28-year time period from 1960 through 1987. But all the signs for price relationships were as expected from the operation of market equilibrating forces on the four determinants--not from the dominance of speculative and political processes. And of the eight coefficients with the expected equilibrating signs, six were statistically significant.

Even though market equilibrating factors generally had the expected impact on prices over the entire period, there is no assurance that these factors caused prices to collapse in the early 1980s. That could be inferred, however, from "equation-

---

[39]With respect to inflation, this occurred only for producer prices. Such a result could be expected from a slower or more limited response to current inflation in the dealer or spot market.

[40]These results confirm some of the conclusions in the metals trade press: "According to some analyses, the changes in exchange rates in recent years have had their largest effect in the copper market. Among metals producers, the copper-producing nations had the largest devaluations in excess of inflation. Low copper prices triggered devaluations in those countries where it was a major source of export income. Currency fluctuations were considered a major factor in making some mining and production operations profitable or unprofitable . . . The strength of the dollar seemed to have been the major factor behind the supply-demand fundamental relationship with price, including lower levels of consumption, higher levels of production, and corresponding changes in inventory that eroded part of the gains in dollar prices" (U.S. Bureau of Mines, *1985 Minerals Yearbook*, 335).

estimated" prices that were similar to actual prices for the 1980-1985 period. Alternatively, large successive differences between "equation" and actual prices, by which actual prices were lower, would indicate that the market equilibrating forces which were revealed in the price level equation for the 25-year period were not descriptive of the price collapse in the first half of the 1980s.

"Equation estimated" prices are obtained by inserting the observed values of the independent variables into the estimated equation for each observation in the series. In fact, "equation" and actual prices for the post-1980 period, as shown in Table Four and Table Five, do not register successive and large negative differences for the years after 1979. The "fitted" dealer prices closely describe actual dealer prices for aluminum, copper and zinc (although "fitted" estimates for lead are too high).[41] The "fitted" producer prices are in most years below actual producer prices for aluminum, nickel, steel and zinc for 1980 through 1984 (see Table Five). The "fitted" producer prices are too high for copper and lead, and are both too high and too low for molybdenum in that same period. But on the whole, those determinants for producer prices in the price level equation result in "equation" estimates that describe actual prices--except for lead and perhaps copper. The precipitous drop in producer prices is explained within the supply-demand framework.

Demand Contraction

How, then, did these market-equilibrating factors work to bring about price collapse? Consider first the impact of industrial production. Shifts to metals substitutes, and new technologies, caused in recent years permanent declines in metals

---

[41] The explanations for the relatively low actual lead prices lie in exceptional recessionary conditions in end-use markets. World sales of motor vehicles declined 12.25 percent relative to 1981 levels. The world-wide changes in GNP are too aggregative to reflect these changes for lead alone. Thus, lead demand declined relative to other metals, and price had declined relative to the others as well. But price convergence had not been completed across the other metals.

Table Four. Differences Between Actual and Equation-Estimated Dealer Prices

Year	*Aluminum*	*Copper*	*Lead*	*Zinc*
		([Po-Pr], in cents per pound)		
1975	-6.27	-18.12	-1.46	-5.57
1978	4.51	4.15	0.36	0.54
1977	1.28	-7.08	6.54	-2.10
1978	0.63	-4.85	3.26	-3.36
1979	17.32	17.78	25.39	4.37
1980	14.04	6.86	2.41	0.05
1981	-1.42	-15.84	1.51	4.47
1982	-0.88	-5.93	-1.76	0.31
1983	19.73	7.57	-4.92	1.84
1984	0.57	-5.99	-0.87	6.87
1985	11.64	-1.68	-5.55	-7.43
1986	19.64	-1.91	-4.91	-2.78

SOURCES: Po, actual dealer prices; IBRD, *Commodity Trade & Price Trends* (1985), and *Metals Week* (various issues).

Pr, the fitted value for the dependent variable in the dealer price equation shown in Table Three, using observed values of the independent variables.

The generalized differenced equation is: Log (Nominal Price) = B1 + B2Log (IP) + B3Log (Stocks) + B4Log (Price Index) + B5Log (Exchange Rate) + D1 (Aluminum) + D2 (Lead) + D3 (Zinc).

For an explanation of how to calculate values of a generalized differenced variable, see Appendix B.

Table Five. Differences Between Actual and Equation-Estimated Producer Prices

Year	*Aluminum*	*Copper*	*Lead*	*Molybdenum*	*Nickel*	*Steel*	*Zinc*
				([Po-Pr], in cents per pound)			
1975	3.75	-5.67	0.62	7.38	30.72	0.76	5.59
1976	2.55	4.50	1.51	51.07	8.69	-0.40	1.34
1977	3.81	-3.39	7.28	48.85	15.79	1.22	-0.61
1978	2.03	3.39	5.06	104.27	-42.42	1.45	-4.04
1979	3.36	14.63	20.75	274.84	49.67	0.62	5.30
1980	6.67	7.64	-1.30	323.64	56.63	2.49	-2.71
1981	8.68	-15.44	-0.65	100.79	13.55	2.53	6.02
1982	5.56	-11.07	-8.17	-250.98	8.94	2.41	-3.83
1983	2.56	-0.34	-1.87	3.68	3.64	2.79	0.95
1984	1.31	-11.89	-2.30	-55.47	-7.36	1.85	4.16
1985	-1.28	-9.86	-10.62	38.95	-121.16	1.27	-8.82
1986	-2.47	-9.37	3.37	-47.45	79.87	-3.17	-6.11

SOURCES: Po, producer prices for aluminum, copper, lead and zinc, Standard and Poor's Corporation, *Basic Statistics on Metals, 1984,* and U.S. Bureau of Mines, *Mineral Commodity Summaries 1988,* for molybdenum and nickel, Amax Corporation; for steel, IBRD, *Commodity Trade and Price Trends* (1986).

Pr, regression equation price, is the fitted value for the dependent variable in the expanded contract price regression equation, using the actual values of the independent variables. The generalized differenced equation is given in Table Three, as: Log (Nominal Price) = B1 + B2Log (IP) + B3Log (Stocks) + B4Log (Price Index) + B5Log (Exchange Rate) + D1 (Aluminum) + D2 (Lead) + D3 (Zinc) + D4 (Steel) + D5 (Nickel) + D6 (Molybdenum)

For an explanation of how to calculate values of a generalized differenced variable, see Appendix B.

demand.[42] To that extent, the price equation coefficient for the industrial production variable in the post-1980 period should be lower than for earlier periods. The insertion of a time-dated variable into the industrial production variable makes it possible

---

[42]Specific examples of metals demand reductions due to the use of new technology include:

ALUMINUM. "... new thinner-gauge can-making technologies ... [and] competition from tin-plated steel and fabricated plastics" (T. Stundza, "Metals Report," *Purchasing*, 23 October 1986, 43).

COPPER. "... new design and fabricating techniques by consuming industries, ranging from smaller-gauge tubing for refrigeration and heating to thinner and lighter stampings for motor vehicle parts... substitutions, especially by aluminum and plastics in the automotive and housing construction markets and by fiber optics in the telephone communications market... a shift in general composition of output from basic industrial products to high-technology products" (ibid., 45). Between 1977 and 1983, downsizing, material substitution and increased engine efficiency accounted for a loss of 15.8 percent of the copper consumed in the automobile industry on a worldwide basis (U.S. Bureau of Mines, *1985 Minerals Yearbook*, 34). "The telecommunications uses of copper account for between 10 and 12 percent of U.S. domestic shipments... However, only about one half to one percent of United States copper shipments is threatened by fiber optics in the short term. A far greater threat to copper usage in the telecommunications fields is the technological innovations which require less copper for the same performance. The use of smaller-diameter telecommunications cables and the multiplexing of signals now have, and are expected to continue to have, a greater impact on copper's use for communications than fiber optics" (Canadian Energy, Mines and Resources, *Canadian Minerals Yearbook*, [Ottawa: Ministry of Supply and Services, 1985]: 23).

LEAD. "Lead demand has been sliding because of technological innovation, government regulatory policy, and the substitution of less-hazardous materials: Better grid-plate designs have boosted the energy, density and life of lead-acid batteries, while reducing the per-unit amount of metal required; tetraethyl lead, the anti-knock additive in leaded gasoline, soon will disappear because of environmental regulations; and titanium dioxide and iron oxide (which are not toxic) have replaced lead as a pigment base in house paints" (U.S. Bureau of Mines, *Minerals Yearbook*, various issues).

MOLYBDENUM. "More substantial reductions in molybdenum consumption came from reductions in unit additions of molybdenum per metric ton of steel produced. Improved heat-treatment techniques in steel-making either reduced, as in the case of microalloyed steels, or eliminated altogether alloy additions... Other developments have enabled greater molybdenum recovery from secondary molybdenum units contained in scrap and have lowered steel producers' requirements for primary material" (Special Molybdenum Issue, *American Metals Market*, 11 July 1985).

NICKEL. "Many plastics have equal or superior corrosion resistance compared with the nickel-bearing corrosion resistant material. Plastic coatings on high-strength steels or other material are comparatively inexpensive. Paint, enamel, or aluminum can be used in place of nickel in electroplating applications. Several combinations of metals and nonmetals are acceptable for use in storage batteries, and can take the place of the nickel-iron and nickel-cadmium combinations" (U.S. Bureau of Mines, *Nickel: A Chapter from Mineral Facts and Problems*, preprint [Washington, D.C., 1985], 10).

to test whether demand has indeed shifted downward significantly in the 1980s.

The revised dealer and producer price level equations are shown in Table Six. Given that the time-related adjustments variables take values of zero from 1960 through 1979, and values of 1.0 from 1980 through 1986, then a post-1980 reduction in demand would be indicated by negative coefficients for those variables. Table Six shows that in the dealer price equation, the time adjustment coefficient is negative but not statistically significant. The producer price equation also has a negative, and insignificant, coefficient for the adjustment variable.[43] The results suggest that the demand function has shifted down during the first six years of this decade--but not by enough to distinguish demand shock from random variation.[44]

Exchange Rates and Inventories

Increased dollar exchange rates have reduced recent metals prices by adding to profit margins for foreign producers on sales in the United States; the increase in dollar exchange rates had the effect of increasing foreign supply both in the U.S. and throughout the world. This is indicated by the negative and significant coefficients for the exchange-rate variables in the price level equations in Table Three and Table Six. Sixty-five percent of any change in the weighted average exchange rate of foreign currency per U.S. dollar has been realized in changes in dealer prices in the opposite direction (given that the coefficient

---

[43]The high R-square and the significant F statistic for the regressions support the conclusion that the extended equation "explains" a substantial portion of price variation. The lack of significance of the new dummy coefficients can be partly explained by the high correlation between this variable and values of the other independent variables, including metals stocks and production.

[44]Individual metals prices have departed from this pattern. Aluminum prices have not been responsive to changes in current industrial production (the price equations for aluminum are shown in Tables B.1 and B.2 in Appendix B, as are equations for all the other metals). Nickel and steel prices have not varied with industrial production, and nickel prices have not varied with levels of inventories to the same extent as in the pooled price equation. But the separate metals have about the same price variation with inflation and the exchange rate as in the pooled price equation.

Table Six. Price Level Equations with Post 1980 Demand Reductions

Independent Variables	*Dealer Prices*	*Producer Prices*
	(Dollars per pound)	
Intercept	-0.1711 (-0.248)	-0.8245 (-3.091) *
World Industrial Production	0.8725 (3.888) *	1.0495 (4.590) *
Post 1980 Adjustment in Coefficient for Production	-0.0210 (-0.711)	-0.0004 (-0.023)
Metal Stocks	-0.1595 (-2.210) *	-0.0667 (-1.430)
Wholesale Price Index	0.3120 (1.964) *	0.3581 (2.943) *
Exchange Rate Index	-1.2333 (-4.994) *	-0.1925 (-1.853)
D1 Aluminum	-0.3908 (-4.397) *	-0.0526 (-0.492)
D2 Lead	-1.1140 (-15.254) *	-0.8231 (-8.152) *
D3 Zinc	-0.9114 (-12.884) *	-0.5171 (-5.441) *
D4 Steel	N/A	-1.1842 (-12.469) *
D5 Nickel	N/A	1.3571 (11.931) *
D6 Molybdenum	N/A	1.9436 (18.848) *
R-Square	0.8551	0.9169
F-Statistic	77.69 (8,96)	163.42 (11,163)
Durbin-Watson	1.738	1.439

SOURCES: Dealer prices, *Metals Week* (various issues), and IBRD, *Commodity Trade and Price Trends* (1986); Producer prices for aluminum, copper, lead and zinc, Standard and Poor's Corporation, *Basic Statistics on Metals, 1984*, and U.S. Bureau of Mines, *Mineral Commodity Summaries 1988*, for molybdenum and nickel, Amax Corporation.

* statistically significant

for exchange rates equals negative 0.646 in the price level equation for the dealer price series in Table Three).[45] Over longer periods, 30 percent of any exchange rate increase for the dollar is realized in producer price reductions (as indicated by the coefficient for the exchange rate index in Table Three). The same results are realized for five of the seven individual metals producer price series (as in Appendix B).

Together, increases in exchange rates and in inventories explain most of the reduction in price levels of the seven metals after the turn of the decade. The other variables played less of a role, even though they changed as much. This finding is indicated in Table Seven. The columns there display the differences between actual prices and those from the producer

---

[45]That is,

$$IER\,(i,t) = \frac{ER\,(i,t)}{ER\,(i,80)} \qquad (a)$$

where t = Year 1960 through 1984, and i is for countries 1 through 5 for the five largest exporting nations to the United States;

IER (i,t) = Indexed exchange rate for country i in year t;

ER (i,t) = Exchange rate in national currency units per U.S. dollar (period average) for country i in year t; and

ER (i,80) = Exchange rate in national currency units per U.S. dollar for country i in the base year 1980.

$$WIER\,(i,t) = IER(i,t) * P(i,t) \qquad (b)$$

where P(i,t) = Production for country i in year t; and

WIER(i,t) = Weighted index exchange rate for country i in year t.

$$PXRATE(t) = \frac{Sum\ WIER(i,t)}{Sum\ P(i,t)} \qquad (c)$$

where PXRATE(t) = Producer exchange rate of a metal in year t;

Sum WIER(i,t) = Sum of the weighted index exchange rates of the top five countries; and

Sum P(i,t) = Sum of the production of the largest five countries.

Table Seven. Differences Between Actual and Supply "Status Quo" Producer Prices

Year	*Aluminum*	*Copper*	*Lead*	*Molybdenum*	*Nickel*	*Steel*	*Zinc*
			([Po-Pr], in cents per pound)				
180	6.00	6.00	-1.00	312.00	53.00	3.00	-3.00
1981	6.00	-16.00	-1.00	65.00	9.00	3.00	5.00
1982	0.00	-16.00	-9.00	-320.00	-16.00	4.00	-5.00
1983	0.00	-7.00	-6.00	-85.00	-11.00	3.00	0.00
1984	0.00	-23.00	-2.00	-84.00	-25.00	2.00	4.00
1985	-2.00	-31.00	-11.00	-156.00	-47.00	2.00	-6.00
1986	-3.00	-40.00	-11.00	-219.00	31.00	1.00	-9.00

SOURCES: Po, producer prices for aluminum, copper, lead and zinc, Standard and Poor's Corporation, *Basic Statistics on Metals, 1984*; for molybdenum and nickel, Amax Corporation; for steel, IBRD, *Commodity Trade and Price Trends* (1986).

Pr, "Status Quo" producer price is the fitted value for the dependent variable, with the two supply variables -- exchange rate and inventory -- constrained to their respective 1980 values.

price equation (assuming the "status quo").[46] The differences are sequentially negative and twice as large as those estimated from the "equation" prices of Table Five. Thus higher exchange rates and inventories account for most of the price reduction.

Even so, during the entire 1960-1985 period there were a number of unpredicted events that caused abrupt changes in the prices of various metals. These were mostly politically determined increases or cutoffs of supply in one country or another, but some involved natural disasters. For example, in 1973 the U.S. Government announced a new policy of stockpile liquidation and sold 698,000 tons of primary aluminum; at the same time, it set price ceilings on most primary commodities for the first time since the Korean War. The effect of these actions was to lower both dealer and producer prices of aluminum. Another example can be seen in the disruptions of the transport system for shipping copper production out of central Africa in 1976 and the resulting reduction in supplies and sharp increases in dealer copper prices.[47] Fifteen such supply shocks were incorporated in the price equation as independent variables restricted to taking two values: "one" for the time of the event, and "zero" otherwise (see Table C.2 in Appendix C). The effects on equation prices from introducing such variables are as expected. Prices are increased for supply-reducing shocks and reduced for supply-increasing actions, with the exception of the 1975 aluminum shock which increased supply but did not reduce prices. Only three of the seventeen coefficients are statistically significant, however. Inclusion of the shock variables does not improve the explainability of the basic price level equation.

---

[46]In this price equation, the "status quo" means that the exchange rate and stocks remain at 1980 levels.

[47]Still another example was the collapse of the International Tin Council's buffer stock acquisition program in October 1985, an event which affected futures trading of all base metals and lowered spot prices for nickel and copper. "The tin crisis broke on October 24, and the nature of trading on all LME rings altered markedly. Between October 24 and October 31, the LME price for copper decreased by (as much as) 5.8 percent as traders made adjustments for the International Tin Council members who were in default to members of the exchange. However, there was little evidence that trading had become distorted to the extent that LME prices for copper had become divorced from the market fundamentals" (U.S. Bureau of Mines, *1985 Minerals Yearbook*, 335, 715).

Supply Expansion During the Post-1980 Period

The expansion of new sources of supply in the last ten years has been extensive. After 1980, these new supplies came mostly from the developing countries (see Table Eight and also Table Seventeen); new sources of molybdenum increased their shares of the world market for that metal from 16.8 to 29.3 percent. Producers of basic steel in the developing countries expanded from 11.4 to 19.0 percent of the total world market over the 1979-1984 period. While shares of nickel and zinc from the developing countries were roughly constant, in part because of concurrent declines in the production from older mines, those of copper and aluminum increased from 42.5 to 48.4 percent and from 11.9 to 17.2 percent, respectively, during the same six-year period.[48]

This expansion in the developing countries has come from new mines that have been fully cost-competitive with existing mines. While labor intensive, they have been built to operate at relatively low energy costs. For aluminum, with power costs making up more than 30 percent of direct operating costs, the new facilities with hydroelectric power sources have had significantly lower operating costs than those in the United States that receive power from coal and nuclear plants.

As they came into the market, the new sources increased their production against constant or falling market sales.[49] That these state-run enterprises were low-cost producers served to delay the supply response to lower prices. The reason is that while the low-cost producers pushed to reach capacity operations,

---

[48]In 1982, "as demand for aluminum continued to weaken, many producers cancelled or deferred previously planned capacity expansions, or permanently closed down obsolete smelters. . . The U.S. and Canada, the two largest aluminum-producing countries in 1950 with 67 percent of world production, produced less than 33 percent of world production in 1982" (U.S. Bureau of Mines, *1982 Minerals Yearbook*, 89).

[49]"Among the major problems facing the U.S. aluminum industry today are the rising costs of energy for converting alumina to metal and the increasing reliance on foreign sources of bauxite and alumina. From the end of 1979 to the end of 1984, the closure of two refineries in the United States had reduced domestic alumina capacity by 12 percent to 6.3 million tons. During this same period, new plants and expansions in Australia, Brazil, Ireland and Venezuela have increased capacity by ten percent to about 40 million tons" (U.S. Bureau of Mines, *Aluminum: A Chapter*, 17).

Table Eight. Metals Production in the Developing Countries

Year	*Aluminum*	*Copper*	*Lead*	*Molybdenum*	*Nickel*	*Steel*	*Zinc*
			(000's Metric Tons, and Percent of Non-Communist World Total)				
1978	1223 (10.89%)	2589 (43.78%)	623 (15.04%)	14.24 (16.14%)	216 (43.67%)	48193 (10.40%)	568 (13.22%)
1979	1473 (11.91%)	2529 (42.53%)	688 (15.74%)	15.50 (16.80%)	253 (48.91%)	56206 (11.41%)	595 (12.67%)
1980	1546 (11.72%)	2617 (44.81%)	640 (15.40%)	17.47 (17.78%)	267 (45.92%)	62836 (13.50%)	560 (12.58%)
1981	1810 (14.08%)	2645 (42.68%)	630 (15.60%)	19.68 (20.45%)	239 (44.36%)	63750 (13.89%)	649 (14.33%)
1982	2000 (17.98%)	2793 (46.88%)	609 (15.09%)	29.50 (34.93%)	222 (50.60%)	65912 (16.62%)	716 (16.61%)
1983	2141 (18.60%)	2896 (48.37%)	597 (15.19%)	25.00 (49.26%)	214 (46.67%)	70011 (17.29%)	774 (16.73%)
1984	2223 (17.23%)	3978 (51.56%)	580 (14.74%)	23.25 (29.33%)	216 (42.56%)	85200 (19.01%)	772 (15.92%)
1985	2550 (20.81%)	3318 (52.81%)	661 (17.35%)	27.30 (32.39%)	185 (34.32%)	89200 (19.80%)	977 (19.69%)
1986	2833 (23.32%)	3190 (46.36%)	699 (17.40%)	26.40 (36.67%)	232 (45.39%)	99300 (22.98%)	971 (20.01%)

SOURCES: For copper, lead and zinc, Metallgesellschaff, *Metals Statistics;* for steel, aluminum, molybdenum and nickel, U.S. Bureau of Mines, *Minerals Yearbook* (various issues).

the higher-cost producers in the industrialized nations continued to operate at levels close to their own capacity, as long as revenues covered operating costs.[50]

The aggregative impact of this supply-side behavior can be indicated by adding a variable for market share expansion to the explanatory equation. Table Nine shows the price equations with a variable for the percentage of market share for the developing countries.[51] The coefficients for this share variable are positive but insignificant for the dealer price equation; they are negative--and significant--for the producer price equation.[52] In the long run, entrants have reduced producer prices by expanding their shares.

There has been some effect from such entry on the general metals price level. If such exogenous supply expansion had not taken place, then prices would have been higher than actual levels in recent years. This is shown by the calculations in Table Ten. Actual prices are as shown in the (A) columns: for 1982-1986, aluminum and copper prices were close to $0.80 per pound, lead was near $0.30 per pound, and zinc was about $0.46

---

[50]For example, in 1985 the estimated production costs of Canada at $0.89 per pound and the United States at $0.70 per pound are higher than the government-owned copper industry of Zaire at $0.57 or of Chile at $0.60. On average, production costs in 1985 were $.68 per pound. As low-cost producers, Chile and Zaire were able to gain market share (U.S. Bureau of Mines, *1985 Minerals Yearbook*, 351, 377-379).

[51]As calculated by dividing the previous year's total production for the developing countries by that year's total non-communist world output, and then squaring the fraction.

[52]The world steel industry made sweeping changes in response to decreased demand and increased supplies due to "the trend towards a geographical shift of the main steel producing centers away from the industrialized countries to the new producing countries of South America and Asia. . . Over the past ten years the world iron and steel industry has taken account of the far-reaching changes which have occurred in its economic environment. It has transformed its structures, plant, strategies, ranges of products and personnel to such an extent that the industry as it appears in 1985 has little in common with the industry of 1975" (U.N. Economic Commission for Europe, "The Steel Market in 1985," [Geneva: UNEC], 5).

In fact "between 1974 and 1983, the U.S. share declined from 18.7 percent to 11.7 percent; the Japanese, from 16.5 percent to 14.8 percent; and the European Economic Community, from 22.1 percent to 16.6 percent. The centrally planned economy countries and the developing countries increased their share of world production. In particular, Asia (including China) boosted its share from 2.2 percent to 5.4 percent. The share produced by the centrally planned economy countries of Europe increased from 30 percent to 37.7 percent" (U.S. Bureau of Mines, *Iron and Steel: A Chapter*, 3).

Table Nine. Price Level Equations with Entrants Share

Independent Variables	*Dealer Prices*	*Producer Prices*
	(Dollars per pound)	
Intercept	-0.8922 (-2.450) *	-0.6773 (-3.104)*
World Industrial Production	1.9096 (5.486) *	1.0051 (4.242) *
Metal Stocks	-0.2252 (-3.274) *	-0.0694 (-1.569)
Wholesale Price Index	-0.1599 (-0.978)	0.4144 (3.944) *
Entrants Share	0.0039 (0.047)	-0.0935 (-2.121) *
D1 Aluminum	-0.3488 (-1.360)	-0.1930 (-1.084)
D2 Lead	-1.0533 (-6.036) *	-0.9046 (-6.484) *
D3 Zinc	-0.8366 (-4.305) *	-0.5754 (-4.022) *
D4 Steel	N/A	-1.2506 (-7.238) *
D5 Nickel	N/A	1.5007 (10.188) *
D6 Molybdenum	N/A	1.9286 (13.449) *
R-Square	0.5327	0.8794
F-Statistic	14.45 (7,94)	127.90 (10,164)
Durbin-Watson	1.588	1.544

SOURCES: Dealer prices, *Metals Week* (various issues), and IBRD, *Commodity Trade and Price Trends* (1986); Producer prices for aluminum, copper, lead and zinc, Standard and Poor's Corporation, *Basic Statistics on Metals, 1984*, and U.S. Bureau of Mines, *Mineral Commodity Summaries 1988*, for molybdenum and nickel, Amax Corporation.

* statistically significant

Table Ten. Simulated Producer Prices Without Supply Growth

Year	*Aluminum*		*Copper*		*Lead*		*Molybdenum*		*Nickel*		*Steel*		*Zinc*	
	(A)	*(B)*	*(A)*	*(B)*	*(A)*	*(B)*	*(A)*	*(B)*	*(A)*	*(B)*	*(A)*	*(B)*	*(A)*	*(B)*
	(Dollars per pound)													
1980	0.64	0.65	0.95	0.96	0.44	0.44	6.46	6.58	2.84	2.88	0.19	0.18	0.41	0.41
1981	0.69	0.71	1.01	1.02	0.38	0.38	7.49	7.85	3.30	3.34	0.20	0.20	0.39	0.40
1982	0.71	0.76	0.86	0.91	0.34	0.35	6.51	7.20	3.11	3.36	0.22	0.21	0.44	0.45
1983	0.75	0.78	0.79	0.85	0.28	0.28	3.61	4.49	3.16	3.31	0.23	0.23	0.42	0.43
1984	0.80	0.81	0.84	0.92	0.29	0.29	3.96	4.39	3.27	3.45	0.25	0.25	0.46	0.46
1985	0.82	0.83	0.79	1.00	0.31	0.31	2.91	4.89	3.22	2.48	0.27	0.26	0.51	0.48
1986	0.83	0.84	0.77	1.08	0.25	0.33	3.61	5.29	2.40	2.89	0.28	0.24	0.47	0.50

SOURCES: (A) Price from the producers price equation in Table Nine with the independent variables at actual values from 1980 through 1985; (B) simulated price from the producers price equation in Table Nine but with the supply variables constrained to their respective 1980 values.

or $0.47 per pound; on the other end of the scale, molybdenum and nickel were from $3.50 to $4.00 per pound in that period. But if production shares and stocks had stayed at 1980 levels, prices would have been as shown in the (B) columns.[53] Aluminum and lead would have sold at two cents per pound more, and copper at fifteen cents more, while zinc prices would have held at the same level. Molybdenum prices would have been $1.00 per pound higher. Only nickel prices would have likely been $.15 per pound lower, if entrants share and inventory levels had held at 1980 levels throughout the decade.

On the whole, the price equations based on market equilibration factors come close to explaining the behavior of prices over the entire period. Not only do the price increases in metals of the 1970s conform to those particular conditions of demand expansion prevalent at that time, but the price collapse of the 1980s also fits with the demand reductions of the later period. The supply expansion of the 1980s, particularly the entrants' share expansion, explained price declines of most metals in the later period. Of the market determinants, the large increase in the dollar exchange rate and in inventories pushed down market prices significantly.[54]

The question still remains as to whether the price level equation with relationships validating market equilibrating

---

[53] These prices have been estimated from the producer price equation in Table Nine, by using only the 1980 level of stocks and 1980 percentage share for each year from 1980 through 1985. The other values of the independent variables used in the equation are the actual observed values.

[54] In copper the normal range of inventories was the equivalent of 1 to 1.75 months of current consumption, acccording to some analysts. It was suggested in the trade press that one aspect of the inventory-price relationship that might have become increasingly important, and which might help to explain some of the metal price weakness since 1983, was the greater role of exchange warehouses as the locations of metal inventories. The percentage of total metal stocks held on the exchanges compared with that held by producers peaked in 1983. It was hypothesized that the closer large inventories are to the market, the more negative their effect on prices. "The more inventory held by producers, the greater resistance to selling at any price. Inventory levels might therefore be the most important guide to price trends" (U.S. Bureau of Mines, *1985 Minerals Yearbook*, 335).

processes is the best description of 1980s prices.[55] Alternatively, negative price runs generated by speculative and political behavior could be better described by dynamic price equations. This possibility is examined by fitting first differences of prices on their own lagged values, as alternatives to price level equations, to see whether they better explain prices.

The Dynamic Price Equation

If speculative inventory-holding dominated market swings, then price reductions would have generated further demand reductions. At the same time, if production was driven by attempts by one or another government enterprise in a developing country to maintain only its cash flow, then price reductions would have generated further production increases. The combination would result in a positive value greater than 1.0

---

[55]A "quantity level" equation similar to the price level equation of Table Three has been constructed by solving the basic supply and demand system for quantity through the elimination of the common terms for price. The coefficients of this quantity equation should all be positive if--with respect to price--there is a negative slope for the underlying demand curve and a positive slope for the supply curve. The fitted quantity equation is as follows:

Quantity = 0.007 + 1.293Industrial Production* - 0.037Stocks - 0.259Price Index* - 0.209Exchange Rate* - 0.067Aluminum - 0.105Lead + 0.035Zinc + 0.205Steel* - 0.049Nickel - 0.159Molybdenum

*Statistically significant; R-square = 0.573; F-statistic = 23.939; Durbin-Watson = 1.737

Contrary to expectations, the stocks, price index and exchange-rate variables have negative coefficients. For the price index and exchange rate, they are statistically significant.

This equation, along with that for price, can be used to estimate the underlying supply and demand elasticities. The ratio of the industrial production coefficient from the price level equation to the industrial production coefficient from the quantity equation is an estimate of the price elasticity of demand (0.311/1.293 = 0.241). The ratio of the stocks coefficient from the price level equation to the stocks coefficient from the quantity equation is an estimate of the price elasticity of supply (-0.059/-0.037 = 1.595).

The supply elasticity derived from the above calculations is positive, as expected. However, the demand elasticity is also positive--an indication that metals demands increase with increasing price. Whether this does or does not contradict the equilibrium argument is dependent on whether particular lags are determinative of supply and whether the elasticity of supply is significantly greater than demand (as indicated).

for the coefficient "b" as in equation 6 of Chapter One: $\Delta P_t = a + b\Delta P_{t-1}$.

The fitted equations in Table Eleven indicate that price changes in one direction did not even have a tendency to continue in that same direction over the 1960-1986 period. The coefficient of lagged price difference was negative for dealer prices and positive for producer prices. The coefficient for the lagged change in producer prices, while positive, is significantly different from 1.0 (in Table Eleven, the coefficient for lagged producer price is only 0.20 and differs significantly from 1.0). What relationship is indicated cannot be differentiated from what would have occurred by chance: These equations do not explain a significant part of the variation in year-to-year percentage price changes (given R-square values not different from zero as shown in Table Eleven).

Still, the question is whether this price change equation better explains the collapse in prices in the 1980s than does the price level equation. Table Four and Table Five indicated serial departures of equation-estimated prices from actual prices, based on the price level equations in Table Three. Table Twelve and Table Thirteen show the deviations of equation-estimated prices from actual prices, where equation-estimated prices are derived from the dynamic price equations in Table Eleven. For dealer prices, the residuals from the dynamic price equation are negative and of larger magnitude than those from the price level equation. The dynamic price equation estimates prices higher than actual prices, and it also estimates prices higher than those from the price level equation (with an error as large as $0.30 per pound for aluminum). For producer prices, the differences between actual prices and the estimates derived from the dynamic price equation again were larger than those from the price level equation (except for lead and zinc). Such relatively large residuals indicate reduced ability of the dynamic equation (as compared to the price level equation) to replicate actual prices, especially for aluminum and molybdenum.

Thus the model based on market equilibrating factors provides a more complete explanation of recent price behavior. Dealer prices in aluminum actually deviated from the dynamic price equation by $0.28 more than from the price level equation. Producer prices in molybdenum departed by similar amounts

Table Eleven. Dynamic Equations for Dealer and Producer Prices, 1960-1986

Independent Variables	*Change in Dealer Prices*	*Change in Producer Prices*
	(Dollars per pound)	
Intercept	1.0424 (0.493)	0.7951 (0.078)
Lagged Change in Prices	-0.0048 (-0.049)	0.2049 (2.803) *
D1 Variable for Aluminum	0.1228 (0.040)	0.9858 (0.067)
D2 Variable for Lead	-2.1961 (-0.733)	-2.5174 (-0.175)
D3 Variable for Zinc	-0.4473 (-0.150)	-0.2584 (-0.018)
D4 Variable for Steel	N/A	-9.2072 (-0.637)
D5 Variable for Nickel	N/A	7.5366 (0.523)
D6 Variable for Molybdenum	N/A	-1.9962 (-0.138)
R-Square	-0.0319	0.0154
F-Statistic	0.190 (4,101)	1.414 (7,179)
Durbin-Watson	1.991	1.925

SOURCES: Dealer prices, *Metals Week* (various issues), and IBRD, *Commodity Trade and Price Trends* (1986); producer prices for aluminum, copper, lead and zinc, Standard and Poor's Corporation, *Basic Statistics on Metals, 1984*, and U.S. Bureau of Mines, *Mineral Commodity Summaries 1988*, for molybdenum and nickel, Amax Corporation.

NOTE: All t-values are calculated based on the null hypothesis, for the coefficient equal to zero. The hypothesis that b = 1.0 is tested by subtracting one from the estimated coefficient and dividing by the coefficient standard error.

* statistically significant

Table Twelve. Differences Between Actual and Dynamic Price Equation Estimates of Dealer Prices

Year	*Aluminum*	*Copper*	*Lead*	*Zinc*
		([Po-Pr], in cents per pound)		
1975	-13.10	-38.98	-6.81	-22.51
1976	6.78	6.77	2.12	-2.70
1977	4.87	-5.00	9.16	-5.61
1978	1.86	0.94	3.19	-0.62
1979	20.49	26.97	26.16	6.41
1980	7.94	8.09	-12.55	0.44
1981	-18.76	-21.00	-7.09	2.41
1982	-14.25	-13.14	-6.89	-4.58
1983	18.77	3.90	-4.89	0.39
1984	-5.07	-10.02	2.13	6.41
1985	-15.19	-1.09	0.16	-9.56
1986	-1.23	-1.04	1.15	1.36

SOURCES: Po, dealer prices from *Metals Week* (various issues) and IBRD, *Commodity Trade and Price Trends* (1986).

Pr, regression equation price, is the fitted value for the dependent variable in the dealer price regression equation. The equation is:
Log (Change in Nominal Price) = B1 + B2Log (Lagged Change in Nominal Price) + D1 (Aluminum) + D2 (Lead) + D3 (Zinc).

Table Thirteen. Differences Between Actual and Dynamic Price Equation Estimates of Producer Prices

Year	*Aluminum*	*Copper*	*Lead*	*Molybdenum*	*Nickel*	*Steel*	*Zinc*
			([Po-Pr], in cents per pound)				
1975	2.16	-16.77	-0.55	25.42	20.37	8.80	-0.79
1976	1.75	6.47	3.55	77.65	2.91	8.21	-2.59
1977	4.12	-4.74	9.01	40.20	3.98	10.41	-3.31
1978	-0.12	5.70	3.20	83.73	-47.61	10.00	-3.15
1979	4.18	17.42	20.53	236.94	69.04	9.00	7.85
1980	6.73	5.63	-12.54	168.96	43.33	11.21	-2.95
1981	2.52	-19.54	-1.97	-163.87	-19.85	9.80	7.02
1982	-3.89	-8.42	-8.17	-424.21	-31.74	9.00	-7.23
1983	-0.47	5.09	3.96	58.40	-3.62	10.21	3.30
1984	1.45	-7.65	2.23	-16.63	-8.33	9.00	5.87
1985	-2.49	-2.61	-4.88	-3.68	-127.33	9.21	-9.97
1986	-1.78	-1.17	5.05	-12.75	135.05	5.21	0.10

SOURCES: Po, producer prices for aluminum, copper, lead, and zinc, Standard and Poor's Corporation, *Basic Statistics on Metals, 1984*, and U.S. Bureau of Mines, *Mineral Commodity Summaries, 1988*; for molybdenum and nickel, Amax Corporation; for steel, IBRD, *Commodity Trade and Price Trends* (1986).

Pr, regression equation price, is the fitted value for the dependent variable in the producer price regression equation. The equation is: Log (Change in Nominal Price) = B1 + B2Log (Lagged Change in Nominal Price) + D1 (Aluminum) + D2 (Lead) + D3 (Zinc) + D4 (Steel) + D5 (Nickel) + D6 (Molybdenum).

from the estimates derived from the dynamic price equation. Even more troublesome, the dynamic price equation fails to describe the full run-up and subsequent decline in the prices of aluminum, copper, molybdenum and nickel. The unexplained differences in the run-up period between dynamic equation and actual prices for these four metals are more than one quarter of the actual prices. And failing to replicate the increases, the dynamic equation does not replicate the price peak from which to measure the collapse in the 1980s. The prices simulated from the dynamic price equation are too low during the collapse in 1980-1981, because the simulated prices of the previous year are below the actual prices that occurred during the run-up. In sum, actual prices in the last decade are not described well by a formulation that has the current year's price change simply following the previous year's price change in the same direction.

Conclusion

There is a part of current metals price behavior that is unexplained. There is no single event that can be said to have caused the collapse--no equivalent of OPEC that adjusted the level of copper or molybdenum prices--but rather the metals market has been subject to simultaneous demand reductions, inventory and exchange rate increases, and inflationary changes that have compounded downward price pressures.

What happened is that important forces came together gradually to cause new equilibrium price levels across all metals. Declines in metals usage rates caused total metals demand to stabilize, even as world production of all goods and services increased. At the same time, a capacity expansion in the developing countries that was induced by the rising value of the dollar undercut market shares and supply restraints by the large North American producing facilities. Due to forecasting mistakes, inventories accumulated. The "collapse" of post-1980 prices thus became more of a "settling" to a new and lower price level.

The alternative explanation gives dominant roles to speculation in demand and politically motivated expansion of supply. It does not work as well, because it does not explain the run-up of prices that created speculation and thereby induced capacity expansion in the 1970s, and it does not describe closely the collapse at a time when these forces supposedly were working in the downward direction. Yet the implications for future prices that arise from maintaining this explanation will be developed in the last chapter.

Chapter Three

PRICE REDUCTIONS IN RESPONSE TO INCREASED COMPETITION

While the price level equations explain more than two thirds of the year-to-year price variation, they do not explain the extent of very large price reductions in certain metals in the early 1980s. An interesting hypothesis is that these reductions were one-time adjustments to newly competitive conditions specific to those metals. An extension of this hypothesis would have it that the expansion of foreign sources of supply into the United States market can be credited not only with increasing supply in general, but, more important, with causing an outbreak of competition in those metals previously dominated by one or few suppliers.

Those supply expansions credited with triggering competition were the government enterprises in the developing countries that built new mine capacity and then put on the market large new volumes of refined product through independent dealers. These companies did not follow the lead of the larger established companies that were selling at producer prices. Rather, they made gains in market share by selling in emerging dealer markets at whatever terms were available. The entrants pushed higher levels of production into markets in the face of declining demand. This action not only decreased dealer prices, but it also ended the pricing dominance in three metals of a few North American companies.

Such an outbreak of competition, if it actually took place, came about only when the producer abandoned efforts--through its own supply restraint--to maintain the market-wide price level. That is, when the "swing" producer was forced into reversing its price-stabilizing policy as a result of further large reductions in its own sales, then competition would inevitably break out. As that producer relaxed its restrictions on total supply, then its additional volumes in conditions of already expanding supply would cause prices to collapse.[56]

To the extent that this reversal in strategy has taken place, then a lower price level would be a permanent condition. Still, it would be difficult to detect. Changes in costs and demands have the same general effect on prices: As costs go down and demands decrease, prices decrease. These changes could be mistaken for the effects of new competition. Also, the one-time price reduction from new competition might take place slowly, in response to the reluctant phasing-out by the established firm of its policy of withholding its sales. In such a case, the strategy reversal by the largest producer would bring about price reductions that would appear to be the result of declining demand.

Certainly price reductions derived strictly from newly competitive conditions were not strikingly evident. There were no public announcements by producers or buyers to the effect that certain metals markets were switching from a noncompetitive to a competitive pricing regime.[57] But there may be two ways to come to the conclusion that prices have been broken down by competition. One can possibly surmise that new

---

[56]An example of this process is the media's description of behavior in the nickel market. "Traditionally, INCO had been the price leader, but the deterioration in the established producer price quote [ended INCO's dominance of] the market in the early 1980s. Nickel trading on the London Metals Exchange (LME) began in 1979, and LME quotations led the market in setting the price since 1981" (U.S. Bureau of Mines, *Nickel: A Chapter*, 11).

[57]To the contrary, Peter Brimelow has implied that INCO determined nickel prices by withholding its supply long after it was profitable to do so. He states that INCO's management was "so insensitive that not only (did) government-subsidized 'social nickel' producers, like Cuba, start up [during the early 1980s] putting jobs and foreign exchange before profits, but capitalist competitors such as Amax and Falconbridge Nickel Mines" also started capacity to gain market share. INCO's market share is now 33 percent as compared to its once prominent position of 78 percent. (Peter Brimelow, "No Nickel Plugged," *Barron's*, 7 December 1981).

competition did take hold in markets that were not only much less concentrated than earlier, but also no more concentrated than others that were competitive in their price formation. In addition, one might be able to draw competitive inferences from newly emerging aspects of price behavior that were demonstrably competitive in nature.

Deconcentration in Metals Markets

As the largest producer's share of capacity and mine or mill output in a market decreases over time, a point is reached at which that producer loses the ability to control market supply by restraint on its output. But there is no general agreement on the share percentage at which "loss of control" takes place. In some markets, smaller firms may jointly cut back on their output in order to help the largest firm maintain that control, even when the largest firm has a low percentage of total output. In other markets the largest firm, even with its high percentage of output, loses control because of rivalry with smaller firms that have excess capacity and expand their output.[58] Without market-share benchmarks for designating when there is "loss of control", it cannot be determined whether individual producer shares in the late 1970s in metals markets declined to a level at which competition could not take place. Even so, very low concentration in certain metals markets would make collective market control in those markets unlikely. The quite low shares of total sales of the largest sources of copper, lead and zinc, both within one country and across countries, make it doubtful that control of supply by one or few firms took place in these metals in the last half of the 1970s. The share of the largest country ranged between 20 and 33 percent (and there were multiple producers within that country), so that single-company control across various countries by 1970 was most unlikely. Much the same can be concluded from concentration in carbon steel products: The sales shares of the largest steel companies were too

[58] Collusion, when tried, is sustained only part of the time because gains can be made by each firm from selling more than its agreed-upon market share. A company may agree while anticipating that it will deviate (see D. Orr and P.W. MacAvoy, 1964, and P.W. MacAvoy, 1977).

low from year to year for them to control world supply by cutting back their outputs.

More questionable were concentration levels in aluminum, molybdenum and nickel. Aluminum production had been more concentrated, with the United States accounting for 45 percent of total world supply in 1970. And even though there were a half dozen U.S. producers, Canadian production was almost as great, and was more highly concentrated (see Table Fourteen). Nickel production at the country level was as concentrated as aluminum production, but it was also more concentrated within the leading country. Molybdenum was highly concentrated, with almost 70 percent of supply provided by the U.S., mostly by one corporation in the early 1970s. (The country-concentration for molybdenum and nickel is also shown in Table Fourteen.)

If copper, lead, zinc and steel were too widely diversified across sources to allow for restricting supply,[59] then aluminum, molybdenum and nickel could have become too highly diversified as concentration in their shares fell significantly around the turn of the decade. They may have experienced changes in the conditions restraining the competitiveness of the market. Particularly, a reduction in shares for the established companies could have led to loss of control in the late 1970s or early 1980s.

Concentration is indicated by the index of dispersion of production shares within each of the seven metals.[60] Copper,

---

[59]Regarding the control of metal supply, the problems created by very low concentration are indicated by the history of attempts to cartelize copper in the earlier period:

"A unilateral restriction undertaken by a Zambian producer in 1955-56 failed for want of cooperation by other producers. A second, more successful restriction took place between 1964 and 1966. After two years of rising prices, price discounting began and the coordination between producers collapsed. The most recent experience has been the formation by Chile, Peru, Zaire and Zambia in 1967 of a producer association (CIPEC). Calls for voluntary restrictions of exports have been made in the last several years, but there has been no appreciable response" (MacAvoy 1977, 24).

[60]Shares for each of the five largest producing countries in one metal, squared and summed, result in the Herfindahl Index value, as shown in Table Fifteen. However the market is divided, the "H" Index indicates the equivalent number of equal-size firms. For example, if five countries were sharing production unequally, so that some have more sales than others, and their squared shares when summed have an index value of 0.16, then their sharing is equivalent to that in a market in which there are six firms of equal size. When there are substantially more than a half dozen same-size mining firms responsible for supply, or their equivalent from the Index, then it

Table Fourteen. Share of Production of the Largest Producing Country

Year	*Aluminum*	*Copper*	*Lead*	*Molybdenum*	*Nickel*	*Steel*	*Zinc*
1960	U.S. 50.6%	U.S. 39.25%	AUSTRALIA 12.99%	U.S. 91.23%	CANADA 77.53%	U.S. 37.52%	U.S. 30.21%
1965	U.S. 49.03%	U.S. 38.70%	U.S. 14.46%	U.S. 78.53%	CANADA 77.03%	U.S. 36.94%	U.S. 29.04%
1970	U.S. 44.74%	U.S. 33.00%	U.S. 20.38%	U.S. 69.11%	CANADA 39.85%	U.S. 28.52%	JAPAN 20.25%
1975	U.S. 35.64%	U.S. 25.71%	U.S. 30.52%	U.S. 67.63%	CANADA 39.88%	U.S. 25.08%	JAPAN 18.78%
1980	U.S. 36.44%	U.S. 23.72%	U.S. 27.75%	U.S. 70.52%	CANADA 33.81%	JAPAN 24.05%	JAPAN 16.49%
1984	U.S. 32.11%	U.S. 20.74%	U.S. 23.33%	U.S. 57.15%	CANADA 34.88%	JAPAN 23.56%	JAPAN 15.56%
1985	U.S. 28.69%	U.S. 19.60%	U.S. 26.95%	U.S. 58.47%	CANADA 28.23%	JAPAN 22.48%	JAPAN 14.78%
1986	U.S. 24.99%	U.S. 20.91%	U.S. 22.65%	U.S. 53.67%	CANADA 33.12%	JAPAN 22.74%	JAPAN 14.59%

SOURCES: For aluminum, copper, lead and zinc, American Bureau of Metal Statistics, Inc., *Non-Ferrous Metal Data* (various issues, 1960-1987); for molybdenum, nickel and steel, U.S. Bureau of Mines, *Minerals Yearbook* (various issues, 1960-1985), and U.S. Bureau of Mines, *Mineral Commodity Summaries* (various issues, 1960-1988).

Table Fifteen. The Herfindahl Index for Country Shares of Various Metals

Year	*Aluminum*	*Copper*	*Lead*	*Molybdenum*	*Nickel*	*Steel*	*Zinc*
				(Sum of the squared market shares)			
1965	0.272	0.176	0.059	0.630	0.618	0.176	0.119
1966	0.263	0.173	0.059	0.558	0.559	0.177	0.120
1967	0.262	0.123	0.059	0.544	0.538	0.163	0.115
1968	0.233	0.131	0.065	0.567	0.489	0.156	0.113
1969	0.243	0.151	0.075	0.538	0.396	0.158	0.115
1970	0.229	0.142	0.079	0.527	0.215	0.150	0.098
1971	0.202	0.129	0.085	0.565	0.200	0.144	0.096
1972	0.193	0.139	0.077	0.549	0.298	0.144	0.091
1973	0.172	0.134	0.075	0.552	0.270	0.153	0.089
1974	0.189	0.122	0.078	0.505	0.261	0.145	0.080
1975	0.153	0.107	0.115	0.507	0.225	0.136	0.070
1976	0.164	0.109	0.126	0.472	0.212	0.137	0.069
1977	0.159	0.111	0.122	0.476	0.196	0.134	0.067
1978	0.166	0.117	0.124	0.507	0.145	0.133	0.065
1979	0.167	0.124	0.124	0.542	0.128	0.127	0.065
1980	0.153	0.102	0.098	0.533	0.168	0.120	0.063
1981	0.146	0.114	0.094	0.487	0.160	0.119	0.058
1982	0.111	0.102	0.093	0.326	0.114	0.106	0.053
1983	0.111	0.091	0.085	0.256	0.123	0.106	0.055
1984	0.123	0.084	0.082	0.390	0.154	0.103	0.057
1985	0.103	0.079	0.084	0.409	0.129	0.099	0.054
1986	0.088	0.084	0.078	0.373	0.151	0.093	0.048

The yearly Herfindahl index was created by calculating the sum of the squared market shares of the five largest producing countries for each of the individual metals. Market shares were computed by dividing each country's production by the total non-communist world production for that year.

The production data series for aluminum, copper, lead and zinc were obtained from various issues of *Non-Ferrous Metal Data*, published by the American Bureau of Metal Statistics, Inc. The data include the years 1960 through 1986. The descriptions of the metal series used are as follows: primary aluminum, refined copper, smelter lead (before 1975), refined lead (after 1975) and slab zinc.

The production data series for molybdenum and nickel for the years 1960 through 1985 were obtained from various issues of *Minerals Yearbook*, published by the U.S. Bureau of Mines, and, for 1986 the *Mineral Commodity Summaries 1988*, published by the U.S. Bureau of Mines.

lead, zinc and steel have index levels so low that there could not have been the capability to control supply even with an elaborate collective agreement. But the "H" Index level for aluminum in the 1970s was between 0.16 and 0.23, which is equivalent to that resulting from the presence of only slightly less than six firms of equal size. At the start of the 1970s, the "H" Index for nickel was at similar levels, although it fell to as low as 0.13 at the end of the decade. The molybdenum "H" Index ranged close to 0.50, a level equivalent to that for a market in which there are only two sources of supply. The largest (or a few larger) producers may have had some ability to control supply in aluminum, nickel and molybdenum.

The "H" indices for aluminum, nickel and molybdenum fell in the 1980s. The reductions were as great as would result from the addition of two more equal-size sources of supply of aluminum and nickel, and also from an addition of two or three equal-size sources of supply of molybdenum. Such large dilutions of otherwise closely held production shares could have caused the breakdown of supply control.

Scrap or secondary production increased as well, and could have had similar effects on market control (see Table Sixteen).[61] The share of total world production that came from

---

an initial hypothesis that is subject to the establishment of mechanisms for collusion, low levels of stocks and excess capacity, and other conditions (see Orr and MacAvoy, 1964).

[61]Examples of these changes in individual metals are as follows:

ALUMINUM. U.S. production of aluminum from old scrap, which increased by 443.2 percent between 1960 and 1976, grew another 134.3 percent between 1976 and 1984, an average increase of 19.2 percent per annum (American Metals Market, *Metal Statistics*, various years).

COPPER. "This above-the-ground secondary [scrap] material represents an enormous supply and is a vital source [of copper] during high-demand periods. Whenever copper is difficult to buy, better grades of scrap fill this gap. Scrap can be converted into refined material at a relatively low price... Conversely, during periods of low consumption scrap can be a drag on the market" (Commodity Research Bureau, *1976 Commodities Yearbook*, [New York: CRBI, 1976], 7).

STEEL. The steel market was traditionally dominated by large integrated steel mills, but smaller "mini-mills" that feed on scrap "... have sprouted like wild flowers across the U.S. in the past two decades. The integrated mills once may have looked upon these little mills that produced steel from scrap as the mouse that roared... [but] the big mills were stung by the price competitiveness that the mini-mills brought to the bar market and which ultimately forced them to adjust their market strategies" ("Metal Capacity Outlook," *Purchasing*, 23 June 1983, 60).

Table Sixteen. Secondary Production as a Percent of Total Metal Production

Year	*Aluminum*	*Copper*	*Lead*	*Zinc*
		(In percent shares)		
1964	17.47%	14.96%	17.762%	6.14%
1965	17.85	16.43	18.34	6.56
1966	17.83	18.16	17.53	6.24
1967	17.19	16.47	18.34	6.33
1968	18.17	16.58	18.65	6.34
1969	18.24	17.38	18.17	7.43
1970	17.85	16.96	18.69	8.34
1971	17.32	15.14	19.27	7.84
1972	18.47	13.75	17.89	9.35
1973	19.05	13.58	20.50	9.66
1974	17.47	13.65	20.94	9.52
1975	18.07	11.17	25.82	8.51
1976	22.15	11.38	26.71	9.11
1977	21.97	11.59	27.97	9.29
1978	22.13	13.60	28.15	8.43
1979	22.64	14.87	30.02	8.32
1980	21.50	15.05	31.29	8.66
1981	23.05	14.06	31.37	9.68
1982	24.77	14.65	30.29	10.93
1983	25.95	14.24	28.88	10.42
1984	22.49	12.88	33.67	10.17
1985	23.67	15.18	37.13	11.07

SOURCE: United Nations, *Industrial Statistics Yearbook* (various years).

scrap aluminum increased by five percent, and most of that came from a large number of quite independent and diverse sources of supply. Growth of scrap molybdenum was not substantial, but increases in secondary nickel played a role in expanding the diversity of production sources in that metal. For aluminum and nickel, the share expansion had an effect on scrap dispersion similar to that from the addition of one more production source of equal size.

That the expansion of sources of supply came from countries on the fringe of the market could have been the most important factor in introducing competition. There were substantial new sources of aluminum, molybdenum and nickel from government enterprises in the Third World countries. The intention of these new suppliers was to produce up to the point at which marginal cost equalled price. In addition, for political reasons associated with maintaining high levels of employment, they went to full capacity rates of output.[62] They pushed harder for more output, even as prices fell, than did private firms oriented to achieving profit returns. An example worthy of consideration is the operating plan developed by CODELCO in Chile for expansion of its molybdenum production (as shown in Table Seventeen). Beginning in 1981, this government enterprise added 20,000 pounds of capacity; in 1984, while world

---

competitiveness that the mini-mills brought to the bar market and which ultimately forced them to adjust their market strategies" ("Metal Capacity Outlook," *Purchasing*, 23 June 1983, 60).

LEAD. Secondary lead is generated from old and new scrap as well as primary mine sources. It accounted for 44.1 percent of all Western world refined lead production from 1981 through 1985. Total U.S. primary lead consumption has decreased by 190,000 mtpy, or 25 percent over the last ten years. However, the consumption of old scrap has increased from 564,000 mtpy, or 43 percent of the lead consumed in 1976, to 566,000 mtpy, or 50 percent of the lead consumed in 1986 (U.S. Bureau of Mines, *Minerals Yearbook*, various issues).

[62]As in the case of nickel, "The Third World countries . . . are to an extent dependent upon nickel sales for foreign exchange, and also for employment opportunities. Hence, they have an interest in trying to enforce steady production even in downturns. But also, as is less often observed, there are powerful commercial and economic pressures to keep production as close as possible to capacity: to maintain a cash flow that will enable servicing the debt, and to reap the economics of scale that are the projects' only source of long-term viability. Thus [public sector] producers have relatively little flexibility to adjust production in the short run" (Robert D. Cairns, "Changing Structure in the World Nickel Industry," *The Antitrust Bulletin*, Fall 1984: 569).

consumption was declining by as much as one half, it added 40,000 pounds more capacity. This required the established United States producer to cut back to compensate for reduced market-wide demand, and a result was the transfer of ten percent of this smaller market to the Chilean producer.[63]

As these new sources began putting their production into the market, there was substantial expansion of spot sales by dealers rather than contract sales by producers. Increased aluminum dealer sales caused spot prices for this refined product

---

[63]The following tables indicate these changes in molybdenum production and consumption from 1981 to 1984.

SELECTED WESTERN WORLD MOLYBDENUM STATISTICS 1981-1984

Basic Statistics

	1981	1982	1983	1984
Production (10^6 lbs.)	209.19	177.64	108.83	182.44
Consumption	159	128	120	145
Capacity	287	305	337	318
Avg. Producer Price ($/lb.)	8.50	4.00	3.65	3.40
Avg. Dealer Price	6.67	3.54	3.78	3.64

SOURCE: American Metals Market, *Metals Statistics* and Molybdenum Special Issues; and U.S. Bureau of Mines, *Minerals Yearbook*, various issues.

Country Shares
(production as a percent of total)

	1981	1982	1983	1984
Canada	13.50	17.30	20.60	14.00
Chile	16.20	24.90	30.90	20.40
Japan	0.08	0.12	0.19	0.18
Mexico	0.47	6.44	11.90	4.90
Peru	2.62	3.59	5.32	3.72
United States	66.88	47.50	30.90	56.82
Other	0.22	0.14	0.18	0.04

SOURCE: U.S. Bureau of Mines, *Minerals Yearbook*, various years. NOTE: Sum of percentages is less than 100, due to rounding error.

Table Seventeen. Production Capacity Expansion in the Developing Nations 1980-1984[1]

Country/ Plant	Aluminum Capacity Expansion[2] Owner	Increase in Metric Tons
Australia		
Kurri-Kurri, New South Wales	Alcan Australia Ltd.	45,372
Tomago, New South Wales	Tomago Aluminum Co.	224,800
Gladston, Queensland	Boyne Smelters Ltd.	103,000
Bell Bay, Tasmania	Comalco	5,445
Bahrain	ALBA 57.9% State-Owned	50,218
Brazil		
Santa Cruz	Valesul Aluminio	86,207
Aratu	Alcan Aluminio do Brasil	29,945
Sao Luis, Maranhao	Aluminio do Maranhao S.A.	100,000
Cameroon		
Penchine-Ugine	Cie. Camerounaise de l'Aluminum	29,000
Egypt		
Nag Hamadi	Egyptal	66,181
India		
Korba, Madhya Pradesh	Bharat Aluminum Co.	25,000
Indonesia		
Kuala Tanjeng, North Sumatra	Asahan Aluminum Co.	225,000
New Zealand		
Bluff	Aluminum Smelter Ltd.	94,272
Norway		
Karmoy Hoyanger	Norsk Hydro AS Ardal og Sunndalverk AS	49,908
South Africa		
Richards Bay	Alusaf Pty. Ltd.	86,700
Yugoslavia		
Bacevici	State	83,485
Titograd	State	45,372

Table Seventeen. Production Capacity Expansion in the Developing Nations 1980-1984 (continued)

	Nickel Capacity Expansion[3]	
Brazil		
Serra da Mantiquerira	Hochschild Group & Anglo American Corp.	5,455
Niquelandia	CODEMIN	5,354
Colombia		
Cerro Matoso	Cerro Matoso, S.A. (45% State-Owned)	20,508
Dominican Republic		
Bonao Dominicana	Falconbridge	3,159
Finland		
Enonkoski	Outokumpu Oy	5,989
Greece		
Euboea	LARCO, S.A.	1,200
South Africa		
Bophuthatswana	Mathey Rustenburg Refiner Ltd.	17,241
Taiwan	Talent Metals Corp.	635
	Copper Capacity Expansion	
Zaire		
Dikuluwe	Gecamines	
Maskhamba	Gecamines	N/A
Dima	Gecamines	
Mexico		
La Caridad	Mexicana de Cobre S.A.	72,000
Atzcapotzalco	Cobre de Mexico S.A.	48,984
Chile		
Lo Aguirre	Sociedad Minera S.A.	17,000
El Teniente	CODELCO	41,800
Andina	CODELCO	6,000

Table Seventeen. Production Capacity Expansion in the Developing Nations 1980-1984 (continued)

	Copper Capacity Expansion (continued)	
Chile (continued)		
El Salvador	CODELCO	16,500
Disputada de Las Condes	Exxon Minerals Chile Inc.	10,600
Las Ventanas	Empressa Nacional de Mineria	56,000
Santiago	Sociedad Minera Pudahuel Ltd.	16,000
India		
Khetri	Hindustan Copper Ltd.	250,000
Iran		
Sar Cheshmeh	State	145,000
Karman Province	State	158,000
Philippines		
Davao del Norte, Mindanao	North Davao Mining Co.	18,000
Isabel S.	PASAR	138,000
Pasil	Batong Buhay Gold Mines Inc.	197,100
Peru		
Ilo	Minera Peru	15,000
Brazil		
Outokumpu	Caraiba Metals	150,000
Caraiba	Caraiba Metals	265,000
Vicosa do Ceara Pedro Verde	Guanordeste Mineracao e Comercio Ltd.	960
Indonesia		
Ertsberg East	Freeport Indonesia Inc.	62,500
Oman		
Lasail	Oman Mining	912,500
Bayda	Oman Mining	365,500
Sohar	Oman Mining	20,000
Morocco		
Bleida	State	50,000

Table Seventeen. Production Capacity Expansion in the Developing Nations 1980-1984 (continued)

	Molybdenum Capacity Expansion[4]	
Chile		
El Teniente	CODELCO	20,065
Chuquicamata	CODELCO	10,337[5]
Mexico		
Cumobabi	Minera Frisco S.A.	13,449
La Caridad, Sonora	Minera Frisco S.A.	123hp
Peru		
Cuajone	Southern Peru Copper Co.	3,400e

NOTES:

[1]All information refers to increases in metric tons of refinery capacity, unless exceptionally suffixed. Data suffixes: e = roughly estimated; hp = high purity molybdenum sulfide production capacity.

Source references include various issues of the American Bureau of Metal Statistics, *Minerals Yearbook*; American Metals Market, "Molybdenum Special Issues" and *Metal Statistics*; the U.S. Department of the Interior, Bureau of Mines, *Minerals Yearbook*; and the Commodities Research Unit Ltd.

[2]All aluminum data are for primary and secondary aluminum refining (sources generally failed to distinguish the proportion of each that capacity figures represent). Alumina is not included. Increases for Australia and Yugoslavia are included.

[3]Smelted nickel production unless otherwise noted.

[4]All molybdenum information in thousands of pounds of concentrate, unless otherwise noted. Increases in by- and co-product molybdenum production capacity in conjunction with increased copper production capacities are not always documented.

[5]Molybdic oxide to molybdenum sulfide, conversion capacity.

to diverge quite substantially from those on contract.[64] In fact, dealer/producer price differences increased from $0.10 to $0.30 in the 1980s (Table Eighteen). The market in nickel in the early 1970s experienced dealer and producer price differences of up to $0.33, but this was small in comparison to the early 1980s when the market producer prices were from $1.00 to $3.00 higher than dealer prices.[65] The beginnings of a dealer market in molybdenum had developed by the middle 1970s, and further development of that market reduced shortages in the late 1970s:

---

[64]Producer pricing was the only basis for aluminum trading prior to World War II. Dealer pricing went into effect in the 1950s, and a well developed "two-tier" pricing system was in full force by the 1970s. In response to increased production by Third World refineries, and by secondary sources, an aluminum futures contract was introduced on the London Metals Exchange for the first time in 1978. On December 8, 1983, aluminum futures trading began on the New York Commodities Exchange (U.S. Bureau of Mines, *Aluminum: A Chapter*, 15).

[65]This divergence was not entirely the result of Third World suppliers being channeled into the dealer market. The Soviet Union periodically releases nickel supply into the non-communist market, which puts downward pressure on Western nickel prices. In 1987 the United States Industrial Outlook stated that although "world consumption of primary nickel rose three percent in 1986 and the production of nickel in the West declined five percent, prices fell. The reason was that the Soviet Union doubled its exports" (U.S. Department of Commerce, "1987 U.S. Industrial Outlook" [Washington, D.C.: GPO, 1987], 11). "The pricing barometer today is the London Metals Exchange price. LME tags are influenced by worldwide stockpiles and periodic dumping of nickel in Europe by the Russians (who sold 100-million lb. last year)" ("Metals Outlook," *Purchasing*, 12 February 1987, 66B9).

The year-to-year percentage changes in nickel production shown in the table below indicate that as Canada cut back in 1980 and 1981 in response to declining demand, the Soviet Union expanded.

PRODUCTION OF REFINED NICKEL IN SELECTED COUNTRIES, 1978-1985
(thousand metric tons)

	1978		1979		1980		1981		1982		1983		1984		1985
Australia	37.3		39.3		35.3		42.5		45.9		41.8		38.7		40.8
United States	33.8		40.3		40.1		44.3		40.8		30.3		40.8		33.0
Japan	79.2		105.9		109.3		93.6		87.3		69.6		74.2		77.5
Cuba	18.3		19.1		20.0		20.9		21.0		20.9		17.3		17.5
Canada	89.2		83.7		152.3		108.8		65.5		87.2		104.0		91.0
Change:		-6%		+82%		-29%		-40%		+33%		+19%		-12%	
U.S.S.R.	155.0		160.0		165.0		170.0		190.0		185.1		194.2		199.6
Change:		+3%		+3%		+3%		+12%		-3%		+4%		+3%	
World Total	599.3		663.3		749.6		700.1		620.1		636.1		699.9		709.8

SOURCE: For years 1978-1982, American Metals Market, *Metal Statistics*; for years 1983-1985, U.S.Bureau of Mines, *Minerals Yearbook*.

Table Eighteen. Producer and Dealer Prices for Three Metals

Year	*Aluminum* (P)	*Aluminum* (D)	*Aluminum* (P-D)	*Molybdenum* (P)	*Molybdenum* (D)	*Molybdenum* (P-D)	*Nickel* (P)	*Nickel* (D)	*Nickel* (P-D)
				(Dollars per pound)					
1960	0.27	0.23	0.04	1.47			0.74		
1961	0.26	0.21	0.05	1.55			0.78		
1962	0.24	0.20	0.04	1.60			0.80		
1963	0.23	0.20	0.03	1.60			0.79		
1964	0.24	0.22	0.02	1.71			0.79		
1965	0.25	0.22	0.03	1.75			0.79		
1966	0.25	0.22	0.03	1.75			0.79		
1967	0.25	0.22	0.03	1.81			0.88		
1968	0.26	0.21	0.05	1.82			0.94		
1969	0.27	0.26	0.01	1.89			1.05		
1970	0.29	0.25	0.04	1.92			1.29		
1971	0.29	0.20	0.09	1.92			1.33		
1972	0.27	0.20	0.07	1.92	1.70	0.22	1.40	1.33	0.07
1973	0.25	0.30	-0.05	1.92	1.86	0.06	1.53	1.47	0.06
1974	0.34	0.43	-0.09	2.30	2.18	0.12	1.74	2.01	-0.27
1975	0.40	0.31	0.09	2.62	2.82	-0.20	2.07	1.89	0.18
1976	0.45	0.39	0.06	3.45	3.73	-0.28	2.25	2.08	0.17
1977	0.51	0.45	0.06	4.01	5.35	-1.34	2.41	2.08	0.33
1978	0.54	0.48	0.06	4.95	9.88	-4.93	2.05	1.93	0.12
1979	0.61	0.69	-0.08	7.50	25.33	-17.83	2.75	2.56	0.19
1980	0.71	0.79	-0.08	9.70	9.63	0.07	3.41	3.08	0.33
1981	0.77	0.61	0.16	8.50	6.62	1.88	3.43	2.87	0.56
1982	0.76	0.48	0.28	4.00	4.20	-0.20	3.20	2.33	0.87
1983	0.78	0.68	0.10	3.64	3.60	0.04	3.20	2.18	1.02
1984	0.81	0.64	0.17	3.56	3.45	0.11	3.20	2.23	0.98
1985	0.81	0.49	0.32	3.33	3.35	-0.02	2.01	2.22	-0.21
1986	0.81	0.56	0.25	3.10	3.14	-0.04	3.20	1.84	1.36
1987	0.88	0.71	0.17	3.25	2.96	0.29	5.15	2.19	2.96

SOURCE: Dealer prices, *Metals Week* (various issues), IBRD, *Commodity Trade and Price Trends* (1986); Producer prices for aluminum, copper, lead and zinc, Standard and Poor's Corporation, *Basic Statistics on Metals, 1984,* and U.S. Bureau of Mines, *Mineral Commodity Summaries 1988,* for molybdenum and nickel, Amax Corporation.

Dealer prices were as high as $17.00 per pound above producer prices. This market was reduced in scale as producers met dealer prices in the 1980s. In all three metals, the expanding dealer markets provided broad access to dealer supplies that substituted for what otherwise would have been contract supplies. The leakage to dealers set up an alternative channel, and metals-using manufacturers were attracted to this channel when dealer prices fell to levels below producer prices.

These changes in market structure and sales outlets could have caused the markets for those three metals to shift into a mode of full-scale competition. Whether that actually occurred can be indicated by certain patterns of prices.

Competitive Price Behavior

Although changes in the 1970s support hypotheses concerning an outbreak of new competition, the proof is to be found in the emergence of competitive price levels. As shares of sales for the established producers declined, those companies should have reacted by taking their production to levels at which their marginal costs were in line with prices. Total supply would have thus increased.

This is to state in the most general way that market prices should have been dependent on the marginal cost of the largest company, on demand elasticity with respect to price for that company, and on the impact of that company's restriction of its supply on the total supply in the market. As other companies expand, the size of price reductions can be attributed to both the largest company's loss of market share and the elimination of that company's "restriction" policy. The formulation is based on the Lerner Index[66], which, in the expression below, relates to those conditions the percentage mark-up of market price over company marginal cost.

$$L=(P-MC_i)/P = S_i(1+k_i)/(E_d+S_f E_f) \qquad (7)$$

[66]See A.P. Lerner, 1934.

P is market price, MC is the firm's marginal cost, S is market share, E is the elasticity of demand for that metal in this market, and k is the "restriction" policy variable. The subscript i refers to the leading company, and the subscript f denotes the collection of smaller companies on the fringe that, in effect, operate as price takers. The "restriction" variable k ranges between -1 (for a leading-firm policy of not relating its supply to total market supply) and +1 (for complete restriction for the entire market supply). More restriction increases the value of k over that range, but if the established largest company eases the reduction of its output in response to increases in other firms' outputs (as a "conjectural" consequence of the other firms' expansions), then k takes a lower value.

The impact of changes in the "restriction" parameter k on the market price level can be measured by the extent of new competition.[67] From substitution and rearrangement of equation 7, the new price level[68] including the change in price is as follows:[69]

$$\frac{P + \Delta P}{P} = \frac{[1 - S_i(1+k_i)/A]}{[1 - (S_i+\Delta S_i)(1+k_i+\Delta k_i)/A]} \qquad (8)$$

If the expansion of foreign producers and the development of a dealer markets cause the established company's decision parameter k to decrease, decreases in price will occur. For example a decrease in k from +1, a policy of full market restriction in the largest company, to zero k, which would imply

[67]It should be clearly indicated that the parameter change in k is not determined by the company's share of sales in the market S_i. Changes in share S_i do not pre-ordain changes in k_i; there is not any average relationship between S_i and k_i across industries. Further, the old "restriction" policy could be eliminated so that a change in competitive behavior would merely be a consequence of the development of a spot or dealer market. Such an outcome is conceivable when several other firms find, for example, that the new dealer market better serves as an outlet for increased supply. An entirely different dimension is how the largest company reacts to the expansion of other companies as the market declines. It is a policy decision that changes k values over time.

[68]This is to assume that marginal cost MC and the large-company elasticity of demand E_d are constant over the period of market share change.

[69]Where $A = (E_d + S_f E_f)$ and is constant over this comparison.

moving to a policy of considering the supply of other companies to be fixed, would bring about a 40-percent reduction in the price level.[70] Concurrent decreases in both the largest firm's share from 60 to 40 percent and in k from +1 to zero would result in a 50-percent decline in prices.

Does this sequence of hypothetical steps describe actual metals price behavior? Producer prices fell with demand reductions and inventory growth, as has been seen. In the early 1980s, both dealer and producer prices declined much more sharply in aluminum, molybdenum and nickel than in the other metals. The particular steepness of the price declines in these three metals can be explained by the reduced market shares of the largest producer, or by policy changes away from supply restriction by the largest producer.

The extent of price cuts, as measured against these standards, can be estimated (as in Table Nineteen). Between 1975 and 1982, producer prices of aluminum increased by more than would have been in line with demand increases, but then fell after 1982 far below levels that would have been in line with demand reductions and inventory increases in those later years.[71] The positive differences between actual and price level equation-estimated prices for the period 1975-1982 are followed by increasingly larger negative differences from 1983 through 1986. Remarkably, the differences between the actual and equation-estimated prices for both molybdenum and nickel follow the same positive-then-negative pattern. Producer prices were increased by too great an extent in the late 1970s and very early '80s,[72] but fell substantially below those levels consistent with demand reductions and increases in the middle 1980s. Since changes in line with the price level equation are the same across all seven metals, the pattern of extraordinarily high prices in the 1970s, followed by sharp reductions in the 1980s, requires an

---

[70]With the assumptions that elasticities of demand are around 1.5 and the fringe producers' share is around 30 percent.

[71]The measure of "in line with demand" is the level from producer prices on the price line equation in Table Three.

[72]Again, an amount determined to be "too great" is larger than the increase predicted from the price level equation in Table Three.

Table Nineteen. Differences Between Actual and Equation-Estimated Dealer and Producer Prices

Year	*Aluminum* (D)	*Aluminum* (P)	*Molybdenum* (P)	*Nickel* (P)
	([Po-Pr], in cents per pound)			
1975	-6.85	3.33	0.08	27.98
1976	4.51	2.67	45.43	4.46
1977	0.13	2.51	44.51	14.28
1978	-0.95	0.57	101.28	-50.30
1979	14.87	1.02	264.83	43.72
1980	10.12	2.77	299.23	42.43
1981	-3.16	6.26	85.10	1.00
1982	-1.98	3.97	-238.65	7.04
1983	17.25	-0.75	43.29	-3.24
1984	-2.00	-3.19	-49.15	-18.11
1985	-12.98	-2.07	-123.64	-134.71
1986	-2.30	-9.02	-120.83	-106.84

SOURCES: D, actual dealer price, from *Metals Week* (various issues), and IBRD, *Commodity Trade and Price Trends* (1986). P, actual producer price, for aluminum, Standard and Poor's Corporation, *Basic Statistics on Metals, 1984*, for molybdenum and nickel, Amax Corporation.

NOTE: Po, is the actual level of average dealer or producer price. Pr, is the estimated price from the price level equation in Table Three, after inserting the average values realized for the independent variables.

explanation quite specific to aluminum, nickel and molybdenum.[73]

For aluminum and nickel, expansion of independent companies restructured mid-1970s markets in which there were the equivalent of six firms, to those in the mid-1980s where there were the equivalent of more than nine firms and a substantial fringe of scrap producers. This should have caused prices to fall in a discontinuous way by eight percent because of share reductions for the leading firms, or by as much as thirteen percent because of a permanent outbreak of competition. Prices of aluminum, in fact, fell by five percent more than could have been expected from demand reductions and dollar exchange-rate appreciation. Prices of nickel fell by 20 percent more than could have been expected to result from similar adjustments for that metal (as indicated by the average size of the residuals from the estimated prices in the price level equation).

The restructuring of molybdenum supply took that market from one in which there was the equivalent of two firms, to one in which there were three firms with a large fringe of smaller sources of supply. Even without any change in market restriction policy, prices should have fallen from reductions in concentration by 12 percentage points. With a significant shift of policy by the leading firm away from aggregate supply restrictions, prices also should have fallen by 30 percent.[74]

[73] It would be very interesting to compare this producer price pattern with that in dealer prices. The dealer price information, however, is quite sparse. Although the series for aluminum does indicate more year-to-year variation with supply/demand factors, there are not positive annual differentials between actual and equation-estimated prices during the late 1970s that are followed by negative differentials thereafter (see Table Nineteen). This indicates that one of the reasons for the departure of dealer prices from producer prices is that dealer prices better reflect changes in supply/demand factors.

[74] Here a policy change is treated as a change in k from 1.0 to zero, where zero denotes a movement to no established company reaction to supply increase from new sources. With changes in shares as given in the "H" indices in Table Fifteen in the period 1980-1986, and A = 1.75, then the percentage price reductions for values of k_i are as follows:

	$\Delta k_i = 0$	$\Delta k_i = 1$
aluminum	8.3%	13.1%
molybdenum	11.7%	30.5%
nickel	2.3%	11.6%

In each case the actual changes in shares were probably greater than assumed. Thus price reductions should have been larger than calculated here.

Actual molybdenum price reductions for 1982 through 1986 below the price level equation are in the 20- to 30-percent range.

Either losses in leading company market shares, with the same policy on supply restrictions, or the elimination of restriction, explains the extraordinary price reductions that took place in molybdenum and aluminum. But both responses to entry at the same time would have caused price reductions twice as large as those realized. Both market share loss and the eliminations of supply restrictions explain the price reduction in nickel.

The price and profit behavior of the so-called dominant producer provides further insight into this possible explanation. The basic expectation for price-cost margins of that firm is as follows: When operating in a period in which the business cycle is moving according to prediction, the company capacity utilization rate should vary with the growth or decline of economic activity. Its profit margin should therefore remain roughly constant. Uniform margins result from operating with marginal production costs roughly the same within a utilization range of 75 percent to full capacity, and from demand conditions the same at various stages of the business cycle--the impact on production and inventories of the level of economic activity notwithstanding.[75] But any change in market competitiveness or in "restriction" policy would cause profit margins to be reduced to account for this new condition. The entry of new firms and the expansion of smaller producers, including the scrap producers, should cause reductions in profit margins for the largest producers in aluminum, molybdenum and nickel (as indicated by the effects of a decrease in share S_i on the Lerner Index in equation 8). Or, that entry might cause the established company to introduce a more competitive policy of supply response so as to reduce profit margins (from a decrease in "k" in equation 8). Either would re-establish the capacity utilization rate of the largest firm, allowing that firm to continue operations as the largest--but no longer dominant--source of supply.

---

[75]That is, the elasticity of demand remains the same over the business cycle, given that the only cyclical change is the number of identical consumers. With both marginal cost and elasticity roughly constant over output ranging from 70- to 95-percent capacity utilization, then profit margins for the dominant firm should stay at the same level over that range.

The actual experience of the largest producer has been similar to that expected. The capacity and production series for leading firms (Table Twenty) show that the largest aluminum, nickel and molybdenum producers were able in the mid-1980s to re-establish capacity utilization rates close to those of 1980, after having experienced large reductions in those rates due to the cyclical downturns in 1981 and 1982 and the relative growth of other sources of supply. Alcan always had a low rate of capacity utilization, in line with its position as the dominant world supplier through a long period of stagnant or falling demand for aluminum. INCO reduced its very high rate of capacity utilization as early as 1978, but it managed to regain operating rates by 1984-1985. To the contrary, Amax has varied between high and low operating rates from year to year throughout this decade.[76]

Profit margins have changed with operating rates, as expected from a loosening of market-share or market-restriction policy. Margins in aluminum, molybdenum and nickel were quite high in the 1970s--12 to 26 percent--as compared to 6 to 12 percent for lead, copper and steel. But at any point in the business cycle in the 1980s, as compared to the 1970s, they had declined for aluminum, molybdenum and nickel by one half (as in Table Twenty-One). For example, margins in aluminum were in the five- to nine-percent range in 1982 rather than at twelve percent as in 1975, a comparable year in the business cycle. Margins in molybdenum were at five to seven percent rather than 20 percent, and those in nickel were negative rather than 26 percent, in 1982 as compared to 1975. In contrast, profit margins for the leading producers in the three other metals industries remained roughly constant over the two decades (except for one or two years, when extraordinary inventory costs from accounting write-offs caused operating margins to be negative for one or two of the metals).

---

[76]After several difficult years in the molybdenum industry, it was at the May 5, 1988, annual meeting that Allen Born, president and chief executive officer of Amax Inc., stated to the shareholders that the company's "molybdenum business has been restructured to the point where it is not only producing cash flow but also profits. Moly is not the shining star it used to be. Those days are gone forever. Today Amax is a swing producer in the moly business. We intend to control our output to keep the market supply and demand in balance, and we will run the business to make a profit."

Table Twenty. Capacity Utilization for Leading Firms

Year	*Alcan*			*INCO*			*Amax*		
	(C)	*(P)*	*(U)*	*(C)*	*(P)*	*(U)*	*(C)*	*(P)*	*(U)*
	(Metric Tons) (000's)			*(Net Tons) (000's)*			*(Pounds) (000,000's)*		
1975	1249	761	60.93%	293	230	73.3%	59.90	59.90	100.0%
1976	1236	793	39.89%	293	231	78.8%	63.70	63.70	100.0%
1977	1236	826	66.83%	293	209	71.2%	74.70	74.70	100.0%
1978	1258	898	71.38%	277	134	48.2%	84.10	84.10	100.0%
1979	1347	709	52.64%	341	128	37.4%	91.90	91.90	100.0%
1980	1426	918	64.38%	331	197	59.5%	102.10	102.10	100.0%
1981	1483	962	64.87%	331	165	49.8%	99.80	94.60	94.8%
1982	1593	917	57.56%	331	101	30.4%	105.20	44.30	42.1%
1983	1619	945	58.37%	304	142	46.5%	110.00	0.00	0.0%
1984	1646	1076	65.37%	304	180	59.0%	110.00	43.60	39.6%
1985	1841	1045	56.76%	304	167	54.9%	110.00	45.00	40.9%

(C) = Capacity (P) = Production (U) = Utilization

SOURCES: For Alcan and Amax, American Bureau of Metals Statistics, Inc., *Non-Ferrous Metals Data*, for INCO, American Metals Market (various issues); annual reports of the three individual corporations.

NOTE: Production for Alcan is only Canadian production. Capacity is for consolidated subsidiaries.

Table Twenty-One. Operating Margins for Selected Metal Producing Corporations

Year	*Alcan*	*Alcoa*	*Asarco*	*Amax*	*Phelps Dodge*	*INCO*	*US Steel*	*Total Industry*
				(Shown in percentage)				
1975	12.15%	12.37%	6.12%	20.21%	11.47%	26.15%	12.13%	14.10%
1976	11.52	15.60	9.00	20.02	14.35	24.19	9.54	10.40
1977	17.72	15.55	5.72	19.70	11.91	15.80	5.70	10.20
1978	19.21	18.24	8.85	23.18	12.70	14.83	6.53	93.00
1979	19.22	19.91	12.39	22.72	17.62	21.14	6.13	12.00
1980	22.65	17.90	7.28	27.62	11.87	24.50	8.02	12.00
1981	15.59	13.55	3.32	19.36	8.21	18.95	9.14	10.50
1982	8.79	5.55	-0.61	5.37	-5.01	-7.80	7.58	9.50
1983	11.27	12.68	5.34	7.21	0.01	-9.41	8.75	2.50
1984	14.83	15.34	1.77	12.39	-4.35	10.35	14.69	4.50
1985	10.16	11.93	4.69	5.78	12.78	20.07	13.70	7.48

SOURCES: The *Compustat* Expanded Annual Industrial and Over-The-Counter file and *Value Line, Inc.,* Value Line Investment Survey.

The operating margin for the firm is equal to sales minus operating costs divided by total annual sales. The operating margin for the industry is the weighted average of the operating margins of all the firms.

The last indicator of a "competitive" shock would be found in the reactions of security prices of one of these firms in the stock market in consequence of a policy change. Stock prices should fall with downturns of economic activity, and should rise when there is recovery, since they reflect the current value of future earnings. But if a firm's earnings level is determined only by the business cycle, then that firm's stock price should move only with the cyclical variation of that industry. On the other hand, if a "competitive" shock can be expected to affect future earnings performance, then those firms that previously had been insulated from competition would experience stock price reductions in excess of those associated with sectoral variations related to the business cycle.

There is substantial indication that "competitive" incursions have affected the stock values of the largest producers in aluminum, molybdenum and nickel. The stock prices of these metals fell by amounts much greater than what could have been expected from variations in industrial and economic activity in the 1980s. Table Twenty-two shows the residuals of the stock prices against the market, as adjusted for the covariance of these prices with the Standard and Poor's 500 stock price index. The three leading companies experienced considerably adverse results against the market, most recently Amax and INCO in particular, as if stockholders had ceased capitalizing higher-than-competitive returns from these firms' operations.

Conclusion

Has the price level fallen permanently as a result of newly competitive conditions in metals markets? Information exists that supports an affirmative answer. The downturn in economic activity between 1978 and 1982 caused reductions of demands which, in turn, caused increases in inventories and decreases in prices. Large and sustained increases in dollar exchange rates brought on a broadly based reduction in prices for the major metals. Prices in the aluminum, molybdenum and

Table Twenty-Two. Cumulative Market Model Residuals for Metal Producing Firms

Period	*Alcan*	*Amax*	*INCO*	*Metal Industry*
		$[R_{it} - (A_i + B_i R_{mt})]$		
1975 to 1977	-10.86%	-24.80%	-41.26%	-9.75%
1978 to 1980	82.96%	10.56%	-20.85%	-8.49%
1981 to 1983	-1.35%	-58.58%	-43.11%	-17.33%
1984 to 1986	-50.36%	-70.21%	-45.74%	-51.00%

SOURCE: Data for average monthly returns are obtained from the Center for Research in Security Prices (University of Chicago).

METHODOLOGY: As first described by Sharpe (1964), the coefficient estimators alpha and beta were obtained by regressing the individual firm or the industry average monthly returns from January 1965 to December 1974 against the monthly equally-weighted market index returns, by using the following price equation:

$$R_i = A_i + B_i R_{mt} + e_{it} \qquad \text{(i)}$$

where R_{it} represents average monthly firm or industry stock returns, R_{mt} represents the average monthly market index returns, and e_{it} represents residuals of the regression. To calculate the abnormal returns, the estimated alpha and beta coefficients obtained from equation 1 are used with the actual monthly stock returns from 1976 through 1986 of the firm and industry as follows:

$$e_i = R_{it} - (a_i + b_i R_{mt}) \qquad \text{(ii)}$$

The residuals, e_{it}, are the measure of the individual firm's or the industry's abnormal returns (i.e., those returns which are different from the expected returns, given the regression coefficient estimators determined in equation 1). The cumulative returns were continuously compounded for the four 36-month periods.

For a more complete description, see Appendix D.

nickel markets were probably affected by an outbreak of competition.[77] In order to restore capacity utilization rates, the largest firms in these industries either increased their production or, more fundamental, moved away from long-standing policies of setting their own production for purposes of holding back on total market supply.

With competitive conditions in the other four major metals already set, metals markets on the whole became more competitive in price and production behavior in the 1980s. This new condition most likely has caused a permanent downward shift in price levels.

---

77 Somewhat contrasting results for aluminum are consistent with relatively less concentration in that industry. In the 1960s most of the world's aluminum was produced by four North American companies. Those producers, along with Pechiney and Alusuisse in Europe, controlled 70-80 percent of the primary aluminum capacity of non-communist countries. There was a larger number of producers in the aluminum industry than either in nickel or molybdenum, both of which had only one key producer (as indicated in this chapter). However, with a number of new smelters operating in the developing countries by 1983, the traditional primary aluminum producers controlled no more than 50 percent of capacity. ("Aluminum: A Rapid Transformation," *The Mining Journal*, 9 September 1983). Relative to the reduction in shares of the largest firms in nickel and molybdenum, this may not have been large. But it both began and terminated at low levels--perhaps too low to allow price control by one or few firms throughout the period.

Chapter Four

THE PERMANENCY OF LOW PRICES

By mid-1987, the commercial and trade press were carrying articles with headlines such as "Metals Prices Rebound". In the July 31, 1987, *New York Times* article of that title, B.J. Feder stated that "rising metals prices . . . are expected to be a fact of industrial life for the rest of this year, according to economists and traders." The expansion of the world economy, along with reductions in exchange rates and inventories, had by then brought about broadly based metals price increases. At that time, with continued GNP growth and reductions in both inventories and the value of the dollar, there was the expectation that higher prices would be sustained through the remainder of the decade. Indeed, one plausible view of the future, based on the stability of these factors, is that a long period of falling and low metals prices has been reserved for the last decade of the 20th century.

This outlook may not sufficiently account for basic changes in the industry. The question is whether higher levels of demand, and smaller annual additions to inventory and production, can be expected to reverse the price collapse of the early to mid-1980s. There are three permanent changes that could obstruct the movement back to a closer relation between metals prices and the business cycle. First, the lower coefficient of prices for industrial production in the 1980s, as compared to earlier times, indicates some permanent shift away from metals utilization by heavy manufacturing in this country. (But this effect is likely to be very small, as indicated by the insignificant demand shift coefficients in Table Six.) Second, those additions to capacity of supply in the metals markets resulting from the 1982-85 high value of the U.S. dollar are not going to disappear in the next five to ten years. Recent capacity expansion in Third World countries is probably capable of providing large annual rises in supply at only slightly higher prices (unless it is for a metal that is a strict by-product).[78] And third: Inflation rates, which, when high, have a substantial effect on metals prices, could bring limited rates of price growth in the metals industries by remaining at low levels in the late 1980s.[79]

At the least, these factors dictate that there will not be a return to the peaks of the price levels of the late 1970s. This can be seen from examining price level changes that will likely occur as a result of changes in the four price determinants. Let's assume that industrial production increases three percent worldwide, that inventories decline 20 percent from 1986 levels, and that exchange rates for the dollar decline to two thirds of 1986 levels. These conditions would be conducive to generating relatively high metals prices as compared to those in the early and middle 1980s. But let's also assume that inflation rates are zero, so that all comparisons can be made in 1986 dollars. Insertions of these percentage changes in the price level equations for producer prices generate projections of 1990 "base" prices that are on average 28 percent higher than actual 1987 prices, without accounting for general inflation (as indicated by Table Twenty-Three).

---

[78] For example, the 15-percent decrease in zinc price in 1987 when other London Metals Exchange prices were appreciating at 36 to 38 percent can be attributed to the supply by one country. China's apparent switch from the status of net importer to net exporter was sufficient to cause a decrease in the zinc price (Economic Intelligence Unit, *World Commodity Outlook*, 4).

[79] Also, current "low" elasticities of metals prices with respect to inflation rates are indicated by coefficients for the inflation rate on dealer and producer prices of 0.05 and 0.48, respectively, in the price level equations of Table Three.

Table Twenty-Three. Projected 1990 Producer Prices

Metal	*1987 Prices*	*Projected "Base" Prices*	*Projected "Expanded Capacity" Prices*	*Projected "1980 Market Conditions" Prices*
		(1986 constant dollars per pound)		
Aluminum	$0.85	$0.97	$0.84	$0.85
Copper	0.78	1.15	1.00	1.19
Lead	0.35	0.41	0.36	0.35
Molybdenum	3.15	4.44	3.87	5.93
Nickel	3.10	3.81	3.31	3.62
Steel	0.24	0.27	0.24	0.22
Zinc	0.43	0.60	0.52	0.51

SOURCE: Forecast prices are from simulations using the price equation of Chapter Two, Table Three; includes industrial production, metal stocks, wholesale price index, exchange rate index and individual metal variables.

ASSUMPTIONS: For the "base case", that industrial production (IP) increases by 3 percent annually from 1987 through 2000, that stocks (STOCK) decline by 20 percent in 1987 and then remain at that level through 2000, that wholesale price index (PI) has no growth rate (numbers are in 1986 constant dollars), and that the exchange rate index (EI) declines in 1987 to two thirds of its 1986 value and remains at that level through 2000. For the "expanded supply and depressed demand case", that IP increases 3 percent annually, that STOCK remains at the 1988 level, that PI is at constant 1986 level, and that EI remains at the 1986 level. For the "1980 Market Conditions" price, that IP increases at 3 percent annually from the 1986 level, that STOCK remains at the 1986 level from 1981 through 2000, that PI remains constant at its 1986 level, and that IE remains at the 1980 level from 1981 through 2000.

Steel prices can be expected to increase by approximately 12 percent over present levels, with lead prices going up 17 percent. Aluminum prices can be expected to increase by 15 percent, nickel prices by 23 percent, copper prices by 50 percent and molybdenum prices by as much as 40 percent in four years. (See Table Twenty-Three, where percentages are calculated as the difference between "base 1990" and actual 1987 prices.)

The molybdenum and nickel increases are large in percentage terms only because current prices are far below the levels expected to have been realized from being exactly on the price equation at the present time. That is, in considering other, more fundamental changes that have taken place since 1980, such large price increases for molybdenum and nickel could be "excessive". Taking account of larger inventories, in keeping with the current levels of Third World capacity, results in predictions for price increases of only 24 percent for molybdenum and seven percent for nickel over the rest of the decade (the "expanded capacity" case in Table Twenty-Three). The prices of these two metals would still be below those in 1980, again without accounting for general price inflation.

Adjusting prices for inflation will not make them higher, except perhaps in molybdenum and nickel (see Table Twenty-Four). That prices in these two metals are forecast to increase most from general inflation is misleading, because they follow from equation replication of run-ups of inflation of the 1970s when each metal was dominated by one or few producers. While sensitivity to inflation varies, as is evident from the individual price equations (see Appendix B), prices in 1990 will most likely be lower than the levels that are projected.

There is an alternative approach to forecasting prices. Rather than relying on these four cyclical and competitive factors, the disequilibrating results from inventory speculation and excessive entry could be considered. The alternative model is that in Chapter Two in which price change is generated by previous price changes. Extrapolating the current condition by use of this dynamic equation provides the projections for 1990 prices shown in Table Twenty-Five. They are lower than the projections from the price level equations in Table Twenty-Three, except for molybdenum, and indeed some are lower than present prices. The forecast steel price is negative, which,

Table Twenty-Four. Projected 1990 Producer Prices with Inflation

Metal	*1987 Prices*	*Projected "Base" Prices*	*Projected "Expanded Capacity" Prices*	*Projected "1980 Market Conditions" Prices*
		(Current dollars per pound)		
Aluminum	$0.85	$1.03	$0.89	$0.90
Copper	0.78	1.22	1.06	1.26
Lead	0.35	0.43	0.38	0.37
Molybdenum	3.15	4.70	4.09	6.27
Nickel	3.10	4.03	3.51	3.84
Steel	0.24	0.29	0.25	0.24
Zinc	0.43	0.63	0.55	0.54

SOURCE: Forecast prices are from simulations using the price equation in Table Three, industrial production, metal stocks, wholesale price index, exchange rate index, and individual metal variables.

The assumptions for the three cases are the same as those stated in Table 23 except that the production index (IP) increases by 3 percent annually in all three cases to reflect current dollar numbers.

Table Twenty-Five. **Projected 1990 Producer Prices Based on the Dynamic Price Equation**

Metal	*1987 Prices*	*"Base" Projected 1990 Producer Prices*
	(Dollars per pound)	
Aluminum	$0.88	$0.71
Copper	0.80	0.71
Lead	0.36	0.25
Molybdenum	3.25	7.81
Nickel	5.15	3.76
Steel	0.25	(-7.63)
Zinc	0.44	0.38

SOURCE: 1987 producer prices per Table Two. "Base" 1990 prices have been derived from simulations using the dynamic price equation in Table Eleven.

although an impossibility, is the logical extension of mid-1980s price declines in this metal. Because the dynamic equation has explained so little of past price behavior, these prices do not have predictive value. But they point to the residual effect of current depressive factors.

Reviewing both sets of forecasts, for market equilibrating and disequilibrating conditions, and for a range of values of the determining factors, the conclusion has to be that prices for the seven basic metals will increase within a limited range by 1990. The market price-setting relationship has changed in ways that work against very large price increases, and, in any event, the expected future values of the key cyclical determinants will likely be of less magnitude. The outbreak of competition in three of the metals seems to have reduced price levels permanently. And speculative factors that failed to explain the price collapse, when used again in projection, only forecast a collapse beyond what has been realized to date.

Extending these projections into the 1990s supports the view that prices will not return to the peaks of the 1970s without the removal of growth and inflation. Based on the price level equation for the year 2000, prices are forecast to be three to ten cents higher than for 1990 for all the metals except molybdenum and nickel, which are predicted to be 20 to 40 cents higher. But once account is taken of expanded supply, beyond the "base" price, the molybdenum and nickel prices for the year 2000 are lower than for the year 1990.

Even a return to the cyclical conditions of the late 1970s--of low inventory and high economy-wide production growth--would not return metals prices to their peak levels. Simulations with the price level equation lead to equation-estimated prices lower than actual 1980 prices under these conditions. This can be inferred from the negative residuals between equation-estimated and actual prices in the late 1970s that imply lower forecast (equation-estimated) prices in the future (see Table Nineteen). In addition, the prices for a "1980 market conditions" case in Table Twenty-Three, which are projections based on 1980 levels of inventory and final production, are lower than actual 1980 prices after accounting for 1980-1990 inflation.

There are good arguments for some permanent effects from the 1981-1986 price decline. It now seems clear that long period supply, such as dollar exchange rates and inventories, and demand factors played the most important role in bringing about that decline. Basic production costs will remain low, given the extensive additions to capacity in developing countries of new mines and plants on line for purposes that do not go far beyond job creation.[80] And the very large reductions in aluminum, molybdenum and nickel prices were a one-time response to reduced seller concentration or increased competition among the larger established firms. As such, lower prices will continue to be realized for these three metals, as well as for the other four already at "competitive" levels.

While there will be price run-ups in one metal or the other, they will be of limited duration and extent. The expansionary forces of supply inherent in large inventories and substantial capacity promise to move metals prices toward levels approximating long-run marginal costs. Competition promises to keep them there for the foreseeable future.

---

[80] The Economic Intelligence Unit states that the 1987 run-up in metals prices was the market's response to the fact that production had been held back while consumption had been slowly recovering. For example, since 1981 U.S. capacity for aluminum, refined copper and refined lead decreased by 32.4, 27 and 14.3 percent, respectively. However, the E.I.U. perceives that price levels for metals will remain low because of the capability to quickly increase supplies. In some instances, production costs are sharply lower when production is resumed, such as in the re-opening of Endako, a molybdenum producer in Canada (E.I.U., *World Commodity Outlook*, 4).

REFERENCES

Adelman, M.A. "Scarcity and World Oil Prices." *Review of Economics and Statistics* (August 1986): 387-397.

Ball, Ray and Robert Marks. "The Economics of Government Intervention in the World Oil Market: Episodic Instability." Working Paper, University of Rochester (Revised October 1986): 1-17.

Bohi, Douglas. *What Causes Oil Price Shocks?* Discussion Paper D-82S. Washington, D.C.: Resources for the Future, January 1983.

Bosworth, Barry and Robert Z. Lawrence. *Commodity Prices and the New Inflation.* Washington, D.C.: The Brookings Institution, 1982.

Cairns, Robert D. "Changing Structure in the World Nickel Industry." *The Antitrust Bulletin* (Fall 1984): 561-575.

Canadian Energy, Mines and Resources. *Canadian Minerals Yearbook.* Ottawa: Ministry of Supply and Services, 1985.

Commodity Research Bureau, Inc. *1976 Commodities Yearbook.* Edited by Harry Jiler. New York: CRBI, 1976.

Cooper, Richard N. and Robert Z. Lawrence. "The 1972-75 Commodity Boom." Brookings Papers on Economic Activity: 3 (1975).

Economic Intelligence Unit. *World Commodity Outlook.* Paris: EIU, 1988.

Fama, Eugene F. *Foundations of Finance.* New York: Basic Books, Inc., 1976.

Fama, Eugene F., Lawrence Fisher, Michael C. Jensen, and Richard Roll. "The Adjustment of Stock Prices to New Information." *International Economic Review*, Vol. 10 (1969): 1-21.

Fisher, Franklin M., Paul H. Cootner, and Martin N. Baily. "Econometric Model of the World Copper Industry." *The Bell Journal of Economics and Management Science* 3 (Autumn 1972): 568-609.

Funkhauser, R. and Paul W. MacAvoy. "A Sample of Observations on Comparative Prices in Public and Private Enterprises, *Journal of Public Economics* 11 (1979).

Harnett, Donald L. *Statistical Methods.* Reading, Massachusetts: Addison-Wesley Publishing Company, 1982.

Hubbard, Glenn R. "Supply Shocks and Price Adjustment in the World Oil Market." *The Quarterly Journal of Economics* (February 1986): 85-102.

International Bank for Reconstruction and Development. *Commodity Trade & Price Trends.* Washington, D.C.: IBRD, 1984 and 1986.

International Monetary Fund. *International Financial Statistics Supplement on Exchange Rates.* Washington, D.C.: IMF, 1985.

International Monetary Fund. *International Financial Statistics Yearbook.* Washington, D.C.: IMF, 1985.

Kaldor, Nicholas. "The Role of Commodity Prices in Economic Recovery." *Lloyds Bank Review* 149 (July 1983): 21-34.

Lerner, A. P. "The Concept of Monopoly and the Measurement of Monopoly Power." *Review of Economic Studies* (June 1934): 157-175.

MacAvoy, Paul W. "Economic Perspective on the Politics of International Commodity Agreements." The Gustavson Memorial Lecture. Tucson, Arizona: University of Arizona Press, 1977.

MacKinnon, James G. and Nancy D. Olewiler. "Disequilibrium Estimation of the Demand for Copper." *Bell Journal of Economics* 11 (Spring 1980): 197-211.

McNicol, David L. "The Two Price System in the Copper Industry." *The Bell Journal of Economics* 6 (Spring 1975): 50-73.

Orr, David and Paul W. MacAvoy. "Price Strategies to Promote Cartel Stability." *Economica* (May 1965): 186-197.

Pindyck, Robert S. and Daniel L. Rubinfeld. *Econometric Models and Economic Forecasts.* New York: McGraw-Hill, 1981.

Sharpe, William F. "Capital Asset Prices: A Theory of Market Equilibrium under Conditions of Risk." *Journal of Finance*, 19 (September 1964): 425-442.

Stundza, Tom. "Metals Outlook." *Purchasing*, 23 October 1986 and 12 February 1987.

United Nations. *International Bank for Reconstruction and Development: 1985 Annual Report.* New York: United Nations, 1985.

United Nations. *Monthly Bulletin of Statistics*, New York: United Nations, various issues 1960-1984.

United Nations Economic Commission for Europe. *The Steel Market in 1985.* Geneva: UNEC, 1986.

United States Bureau of Mines. *Aluminum: A Chapter from Mineral Facts and Problems.* Preprint. Washington, D.C.: Department of the Interior, 1985.

United States Bureau of Mines. *Copper: A Chapter from Mineral Facts and Problems.* Preprint. Washington, D.C.: Department of the Interior, 1985.

United States Bureau of Mines. *Iron and Steel: A Chapter from Mineral Facts and Problems.* Preprint. Washington, D.C.: Department of the Interior, 1985.

United States Bureau of Mines. *Nickel: A Chapter from Mineral Facts and Problems.* Preprint. Washington, D.C.: Department of the Interior, 1985.

United States Bureau of Mines. *1986 Minerals Yearbook.* Preprint. Washington, D.C.: Department of the Interior, 1987.

United States Bureau of Mines. *1985 Minerals Yearbook.* Vol. I. Washington, D.C.: Department of the Interior, 1987.

United States Bureau of Mines. *1982 Minerals Yearbook.* Vol. I. Washington, D.C.: Department of the Interior, 1984.

United States Bureau of Mines. *1980 Minerals Yearbook.* Vol. I. Washington, D.C.: Department of the Interior, 1982.

United States Department of Commerce. *1987 U.S. Industrial Outlook.* Washington, D.C.: General Printing Office, 1987.

United States International Trade Commission. *Annual Survey Concerning Competitive Conditions in the Steel Industry.* Washington, D.C.: USITC, September 1986.

Verleger, Philip K. "The Determinants of Official OPEC Crude Prices." *Review of Economics and Statistics* LXIV (May 1982): 177-183.

Walde, Thomas. "World Mineral Development: Current Issues." *Columbia Journal of World Business* 19 (Spring 1984): 27-34.

Appendix A

DATA SOURCES

Data on non-communist world industrial production have been obtained from various issues of the "Monthly Bulletin of Statistics", a United Nations publication. An index of industrial production was then developed for the years 1960 through 1986, with 1980 as the base year. The average annual change in the industrial production index during this period was 3.9 percent. Fluctuations greater than one standard deviation from this average occurred in the years 1964, 1967, 1969, 1970, 1973 through 1976, 1980 through 1983, 1985 and 1986.

The price series for aluminum, copper, lead and zinc were obtained from the Standard and Poor's Corporation publication *Basic Statistics on Metals, 1986*. The Amax Corporation was the source of the price data on molybdenum and nickel, from series compiled on contract by Data Resources, Inc.

Aluminum prices increased at an average annual rate of 4.7 percent from 1960 through 1986. In 1963, 1969, 1973 and 1975, various supply shocks in the aluminum market were observed. In 1963, the U.S. Government instituted a program to dispose of 135,000 short tons of aluminum from its stockpile by 1965. In 1969, two major U.S. aluminum producers were involved in strikes that led to extraordinarily low aluminum inventory levels. In 1973, the U.S. Government released 698,000 short tons of primary aluminum from its inventories. Federal price controls on aluminum in 1975 and 1978 had the effect of retarding the growth of aluminum prices.

Copper prices grew at an average annual rate of 3.6 percent from 1960 to 1986. Shocks in 1965 and 1976 were introduced into the basic market for copper supply. In 1965, the release of 120,000 tons of copper from U.S. Government inventories placed increased downward pressure on copper prices. Disruption of transport systems utilized by copper producers in central Africa resulted in supply reductions in 1976.

The average annual rate of change in the price of lead from 1960 to 1986 was 4.2 percent. Exogenous supply disruptions affecting nominal lead prices occurred in 1964, 1973, 1979 and 1982. Increased nationalization of lead mines in Africa, coupled with existing labor troubles at Australian production sites, resulted in supply reductions in 1964. Price controls in effect in the U.S. retarded the growth of lead prices in 1973. In 1979, plant shutdowns by lead manufacturers in the U.S. Midwest led to inventory reductions. In 1979 and 1982, new environmental regulations were introduced in the U.S. that caused significant future reductions in demand.

Molybdenum prices varied by 4.8 percent annually from 1960 through 1986. Shock conditions were present in 1973 and 1974. Disposal of large quantities of molybdenum from U.S. Government stockpiles during 1973 and 1974 increased supply. Because molybdenum is a by-product of copper mining, changes in copper output have significantly affected molybdenum supply.

Prices for nickel increased at an average annual rate of 7.1 percent from 1960 to 1986. Supply disruptions exogenous to the market were likely experienced in 1970, 1980 and 1981. A Canadian labor strike in 1969 resulted in a shortage of nickel in 1970. Taxes on nickel sales were introduced in 1980 by U.S. environmental authorities. An emissions control order was put into effect in Canada in 1981.

Prices in the zinc market increased at an average rate of 5.7 percent annually from 1960 to 1986. During the years 1974, 1976, 1977 and 1980, various political factors can be counted as having had market impacts. The removal of U.S. price controls and decreased worldwide capacity in 1974 resulted in a reduced supply for that year. A decrease in the U.S. Government stockpile goal for zinc caused actual market supply to increase unexpectedly in 1976. Strikes and mine closings throughout the U.S. and Canada resulted in a lower-than-predicted supply in 1977. A 1980 reduction in the stockpile goal, and an unexpectedly large rise in output from various mines, led to an increase in the zinc supply.

Appendix B

STATISTICAL PROCEDURES FOR FITTING THE PRICE LEVEL EQUATIONS

In a regression model, one of the critical assumptions is that equation residuals are mutually independent. But with time series data used to fit the regression equation, it is common to observe that successive residuals are correlated. Such serial correlation does not affect bias or the consistency of ordinary least-squares regression estimators, but it does affect their efficiency. In the case of positive serial correlation, estimates of the standard errors of computed coefficients are smaller than the true standard errors, which leads to conclusions that the regression coefficients are more significant statistically than they actually are. For negative autocorrelation, standard errors are larger, leading in some cases to the conclusion that the parameter estimates are insignificant when they are not.

The most widely used test for serial correlation is the Durbin-Watson (DW) test, with unacceptable values of the DW statistic in the 0-to-1 range. The residuals in our ordinary least-squares price level equations, for both dealer and producer metal prices, were positively correlated and had Durbin-Watson statistic values in the unacceptable range. Since the economic interpretation of the results in the equations depended on the significance of the coefficients, certain serial statistical transformations were conducted to remove the serial correlation of residuals.

Specifically, "generalized differencing" was used to adjust the OLS regression estimates so that the resulting equations would be more efficient. This procedure involves altering the regression model. The critical assumption underlying this transformation is that ρ--the autocorrelation coefficient--is known or has been estimated close to its true value. The OLS regression equation is transformed by multiplying the one-year lagged values of the dependent and independent variables by the estimated ρ. These variables are then subtracted from the current values of the dependent and independent variables. The following transformed equation is then estimated:

$$Y_t^* = B_1 (1-\rho) + B_2X_{2t}^* + B_3X_{3t}^* + B_4X_{4t}^* + B_5X_{5t}^* + v_t$$

where

$$Y_t^* = Y_t - \rho Y_{t-1} \qquad X_{2t}^* = X_{2t} - \rho X_{2t-1}$$
$$X_{3t}^* = X_{3t} - \rho X_{3t-1} \qquad X_{4t}^* = X_{4t} - \rho X_{4t-1}$$
$$X_{5t}^* = X_{5t} - \rho X_{5t-1} \qquad v_t = e_t - \rho e_{t-1}$$

By construction, the transformed equation has an error process that is independently distributed with zero mean and constant variance. Thus OLS regression estimation procedures applied to the transformed variables yield efficient estimates of all the parameters.

The results of generalized differencing for the transformed individual price level equations are shown in Tables B.1 and B.2, for data series from 1960 to 1986. They indicate that:

> Metals prices are responsive to economic activity: A higher level of economic growth causes demand for metals to increase, which, in turn, causes metals prices to increase. However, aluminum and steel producer prices have not increased with economic activity in this way (due to correlation of the industrial production variable with other independent variables).

> World metals prices are negatively related to metals inventories (or stocks). An increase in metals

inventories from the level of the previous year implies excess supply. Metals producers liquidating these stocks add to amounts available on the dealer market; prices are thus lowered to the point where the marginal benefit from decreased holding costs is equal to the marginal profit loss from reduced prices.

Metals prices increase with the wholesale (or general) price index, in a manner that parallels inflation and indicates the prices of metals substitutes.

Nominal metals prices decline with increases in the dollar exchange rate. Prices are determined in the geographical center of the market, which is the United States. Thus increases in the value of U.S. currency cause costs to decrease for those suppliers who pay for inputs in a foreign currency. This cost reduction against constant nominal revenue increases supply, which pushes prices down. In the two tables for producer and dealer prices, the coefficient for the exchange rate variable has a negative sign for all except one of the metals and is statistically significant for five of the eleven cases.

Table B.1. Individual Metal Equations for Producer Prices

Independent Variable	*Aluminum*	*Copper*	*Lead*	*Molybdenum*	*Nickel*	*Steel*	*Zinc*
			(Dollars per pound)				
Intercept	0.4848 (1.315)	-0.2268 (-0.433)	-1.1279 (-0.932)	-0.5142 (-0.414)	-0.7640 (-0.313)	-2.4416 (-5.728) *	-1.1000 (-1.631)
World Industrial Production	-0.0868 (-0.366)	0.7636 (3.301) *	1.4821 (1.937)	0.9848 (1.621)	0.7422 (0.964)	-0.5683 (-0.948)	0.8950 (1.582)
Metal Stocks	-0.0088 (-0.252)	-0.482 (-0.792)	-0.1096 (-0.612)	-0.3909 (-2.875) *	-0.0363 (-0.287)	-.8256 (1.750)	0.0141 (0.082)
Wholesale Price Index	0.7636 (8.340) *	0.3063 (2.384) *	-0.0857 (-0.328)	0.9553 (3.870) *	0.7344 (2.316) *	0.9978 (6.131) *	0.4609 (2.425) *
Exchange Rate Index	-0.2340 (-0.430)	-0.7191 (-3.628) *	-0.3050 (-0.358)	-0.8762 (-5.248) *	-1.4334 (-2.049) *	0.0170 (0.061)	0.7149 (1.203)
R-Square	0.918	0.9178	0.3344	0.7964	0.8512	0.9779	0.6952
F-Statistic	70.98 (4,21)	70.786 (4,21)	4.014 (4,20)	24.468 (4,20)	29.59 (4,16)	277.513 (4,21)	15.254 (4,21)
Durbin-Watson Statistic	0.887	1.849	1.248	1.848	1.895	1.408	1.226

SOURCE: Producer prices for aluminum, copper, lead and zinc, Standard and Poor's Corporation, *Basic Statistics on Metals*, 1985; for molybdenum and nickel, Amax Corporation; for steel, IBRD, *Commodity Trade and Price Trends* (1986).

* Statistically significant at .05 level.

Table B.2. Individual Metal Equations for Dealer Prices

Independent Variable	*Aluminum*	*Copper*	*Lead*	*Zinc*
		(Dollars per pound)		
Intercept	2.1259 (3.026) *	-0.4434 (-0.489)	-2.2438 (-1.506)	-2.4069 (-2.214) *
World Industrial Production	-0.1728 (-1.082)	1.4198 (2.886) *	1.9076 (2.775) *	2.3312 (2.681) *
Metal Stocks	-0.1176 (-2.137) *	-0.2541 (-2.154) *	-0.0098 (-0.045)	-0.2058 (-0.749)
Wholesale Price Index	0.8139 (10.982) *	-0.0716 (-0.277)	-0.3150 (-1.271)	-0.1035 (-0.351)
Exchange Rate Index	-3.1339 (-5.955) *	-0.4435 (-1.170)	-1.9137 (-2.013) *	-0.4206 (-0.440)
R-Square	0.9614	0.5646	0.5409	0.4954
F-Statistic	144.05 (4,19)	9.106 (4,21)	8.069 (4,20)	7.14 (4,21)
Durbin-Watson Statistic	2.092	1.691	1.478	1.350

SOURCE: Dealer prices, IBRD, *Commodity Trade and Price Trends* (1986).

* Statistically significant at the .05 level.

Chart B.1. Aluminum - Dealer Price, Basic Equation

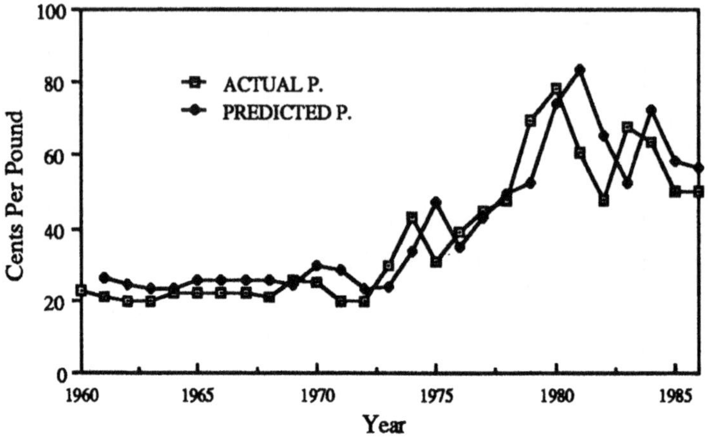

Price = 2.13 - 0.17 IP - 0.12 Stocks + 0.81 PIndex - 3.13 XRate
(3.026) (-1.082) (-2.137) (10.982) (-5.955)

R Square = 0.9614

Chart B.2. Aluminum - Producer Price, Basic Equation

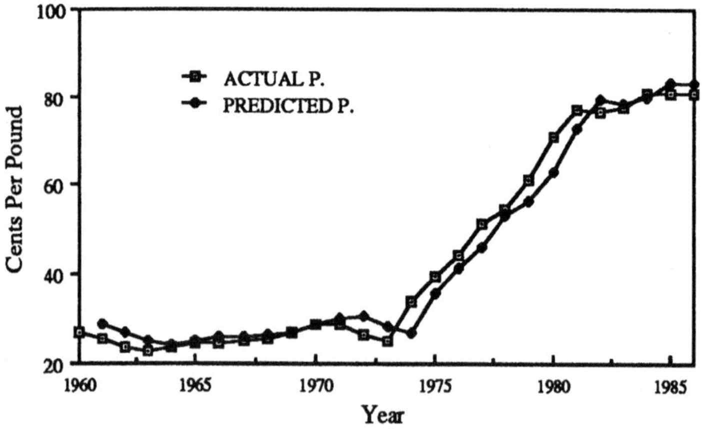

Price = 0.49 - 0.09 IP - 0.01 Stocks + 0.76 PIndex - 0.23 XRate
(1.315) (-0.366) (-0.252) (8.340) (-0.430)

R Square = 0.9180

Chart B.3. Copper - Dealer Price, Basic Equation

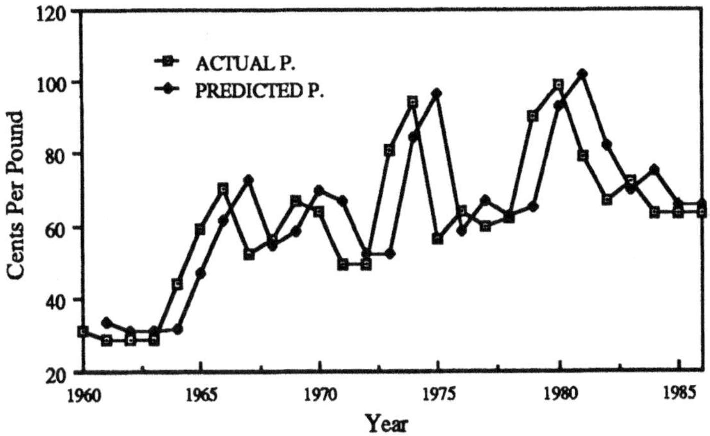

Price = - 0.44 + 1.42 IP - 0.25 Stocks - 0.07 PIndex - 0.44 XRate
(-0.489) (2.886) (-2.154) (-0.277) (-1.170)

R Square = 0.5646

Chart B.4. Copper - Producer Price, Basic Equation

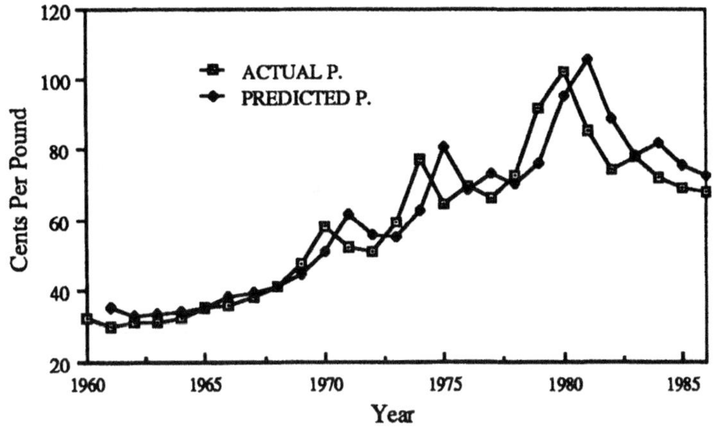

Price = -0.23 + 0.76 IP - 0.05 Stocks + 0.31 PIndex - 0.72 XRate
(-0.433) (3.301) (-0.792) (2.384) (-3.628)

R Square = 0.9178

Chart B.5. Lead - Dealer Price, Basic Equation

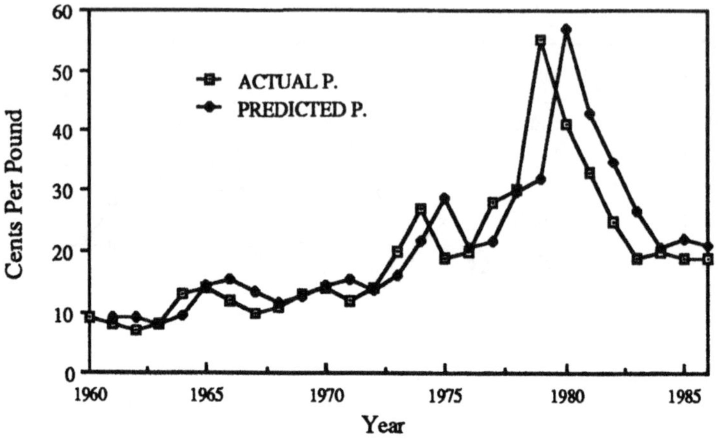

Price = - 2.24 + 1.91 IP - 0.01 Stocks - 0.32 PIndex - 1.91 XRate
(-1.506) (2.775) (-0.045) (-1.271) (-2.013)

R Square = 0.5409

Chart B.6. Lead - Producer Price, Basic Equation

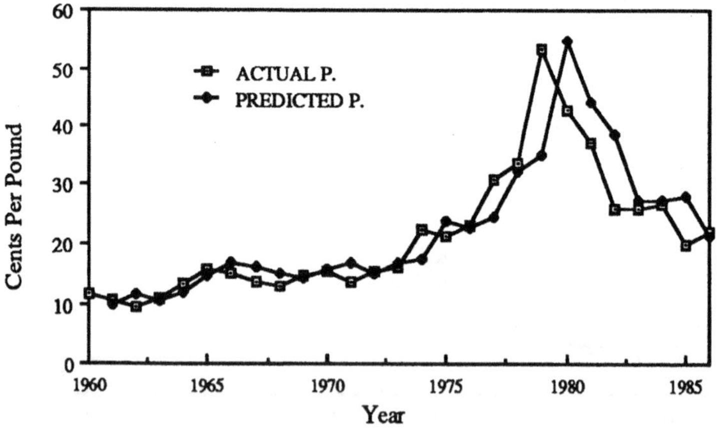

Price = -1.13 + 1.48 IP - 0.11 Stocks - 0.09 PIndex - 0.31 XRate
(-0.932) (1.937) (-0.612) (-0.328) (-0.358)

R Square = 0.3344

Chart B.7. Zinc - Dealer Price, Basic Equation

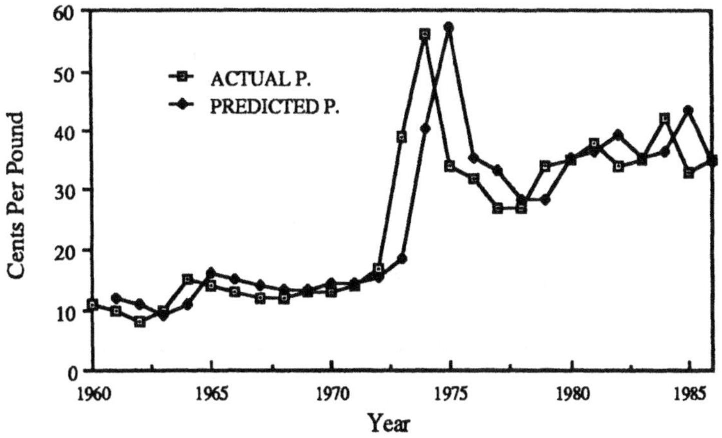

Price = - 2.41 + 2.33 IP - 0.21 Stocks - 0.10 PIndex - 0.42 XRate
(-2.214) (2.681) (-0.749) (-0.351) (-0.440)

R Square = 0.4954

Chart B.8. Zinc - Producer Price, Basic Equation

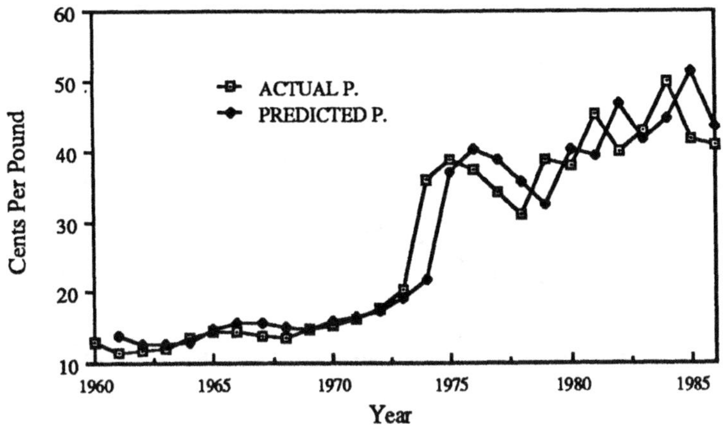

Price = -1.10+ 0.90 IP + 0.01Stocks + 0.46 PIndex + 0.72 XRate
(-1.631) (1.582) (0.082) (2.425) (1.103)

R Square = 0.6952

Chart B.9. Molybdenum - Producer Price, Basic Equation

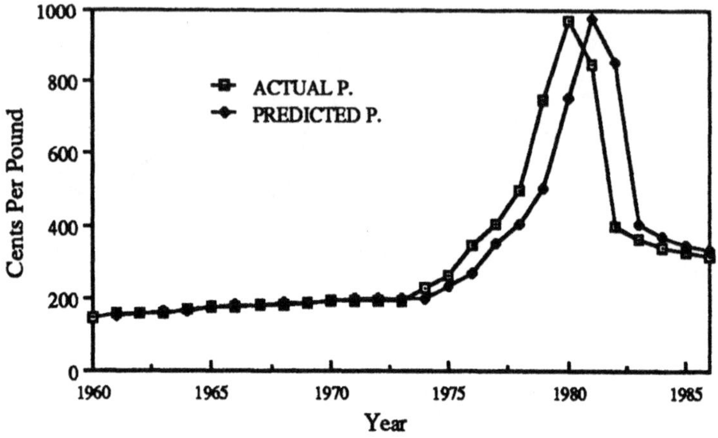

Price = -0.51 + 0.99 IP - 0.39 Stocks + 0.96 PIndex - 0.88 XRate
(-0.414) (1.621) (-2.875) (3.870) (-5.248)

R Square = 0.7964

Chart B.10. Nickel - Producer Price, Basic Equation

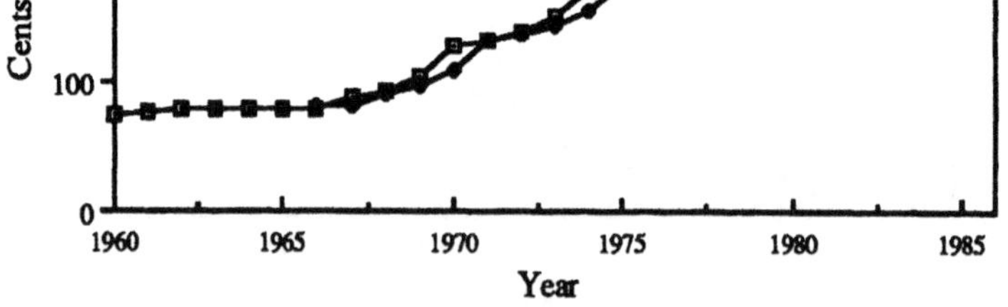

Price = -0.76 + 0.74 IP - 0.04 Stocks + 0.73 PIndex - 1.43 XRate
(-0.373) (0.964) (-0.287) (2.316) (-2.049)

R Square = 0.8512

Chart B.11. Steel - Producer Price, Basic Equation

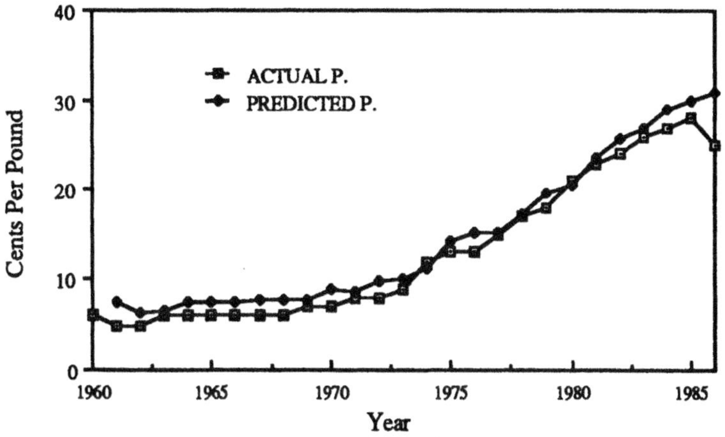

Price = -2.44 - 0.57 IP+ 0.83 Stocks + 0.99 PIndex + 0.02 XRate
(-5.728) (-0.946) (1.750) (6.131) (0.061)

R Square = 0.9779

Appendix C

MARKET SUPPLY SHOCKS

From 1960 through 1986 there were certain disruptions in the individual metals markets that were caused by political decisions, acts of nature or some other factors that have not been explicitly included in our "supply/demand" model. These exogenous supply shocks for the period of the study are identified for the individual metals in Table C.1. In a regression equation, these exogenous supply shocks can be modeled by the inclusion of dummy variables which take on a value of 1 for the year of the shock and zero otherwise. The fifteen dummy variables are added to the pooled price level equation of Table Three. Table C.2 contains the results for the regression model for both producer and dealer metals prices with the inclusion of these dummy variables.

Table C.1. Metal Supply Shocks

Aluminum	
1963:	The U.S. Government institutes a program to dispose of 135,000 short tons of aluminum by mid-1965; 51,589 tons are sold in 1963.
1973:	698,800 short tons of primary aluminum shipped from U.S. Government inventories.
1975:	2,486 tons of primary aluminum shipped from U.S. Government inventories. Price increases for primary aluminum ingot delayed until August by the Council on Wage and Price Stability.
Copper	
1965:	120,000 tons of copper released from U.S. Government inventories.
1976:	The transport system used by producers in central Africa is disrupted.
Lead	
1964:	Production in Africa decreases due to nationalization of some mines.
1972:	U.S. Government price controls go into effect until December of 1973.
1973:	U.S. Government stockpile objective for lead is reduced, as 211,541 tons is withdrawn from producer and government stocks. The U.S. lead price advanced to a record high in 1974 following the removal of price controls in December 1973.

Table C.1. Metal Supply Shocks (continued)

Lead (continued)	
1982:	Revised Environmental Protection Agency (EPA) regulations concerning the use of lead in gasoline become effective. The new standard is 1.10 grams per gallon absolute limit for all leaded gasoline, including imports, with no exceptions for small refiners after July 1, 1983.
Molybdenum	
1973:	36.5 million pounds of molybdenum from U.S. Government stockpile authorized for disposal.
1974:	35 million pounds of molybdenum shipped from U.S. Government stockpile.
Nickel	
1970:	Canadian labor strike reduces supply; most of the industry is affected in the early part of the year.
1980:	The "Superfund Act" authorizes a $0.225 tax per pound of pure nickel produced in or brought into the United States.
Zinc	
1976:	Increase in the U.S. Government stockpile goal for zinc from 374,830 tons to 1,313,000 tons eliminates any excess for disposal.
1980:	U.S. Government stockpile goal is reduced from 1,313,000 tons to 1,292,739 tons.

Table C.2. Price Level Equations with Supply Shocks

Independent Variable	*Dealer Prices*	*Producer Prices*
	(Dollars per pound)	
Intercept	-0.5556 (-5.598) *	0.2832 (1.315)
World Industrial Production	2.2765 (6.062) *	0.4034 (2.174) *
Metal Stocks	-0.1603 (-2.623) *	-0.0684 (-1.620)
Wholesale Price Index	0.2316 (1.248)	0.4751 (5.823) *
Exchange Rate Index	0.4480 (2.869) *	-0.3640 (-4.051) *
D1 Variable Aluminum	-1.2054 (-2.115) *	-0.2960 (-2.801) *
D2 Variable Lead	-3.7688 (-8.035) *	-1.0960 (-10.569) *
D3 Variable Zinc	-1.9668 (-7.441) *	-0.8008 (-9.152) *
D4 Variable Steel	N/A	-1.5774 (-16.921) *
D5 Variable Nickel	N/A	1.0995 (9.925) *
D6 Variable Molybdenum	N/A	1.6287 (15.760) *
D7 1963 Aluminum	-0.0208 (-0.090)	-0.0753 (-0.499)
D9 1973 Aluminum	0.1740 (0.751)	-0.2643 (-1.742)
D10 1975 Aluminum	-0.0681 (-0.291)	0.0788 (0.523)

Table C.2. Price Level Equations with Supply Shocks (continued)

D11 1964 Lead	0.6684 (2.884) *	0.2081 (1.355)
D24 1972 Lead	0.2274 (1.994)	0.0259 (0.171)
D12 1973 Lead	0.4076 (1.788)	-0.0723 (-0.478)
D25 1982 Lead	-0.0444 (-0.192)	-0.2659 (-1.757)
D15 1976 Zinc	-0.0643 (-0.282)	0.0641 (0.425)
D17 1980 Zinc	0.0192 (0.084)	-0.0649 (-0.432)
D18 1965 Copper	0.1481 (0.650)	-0.0128 (-0.085)
D19 1976 Copper	0.0046 (0.020)	0.0686 (0.447)
D20 1970 Nickel	N/A	0.0786 (0.515)
D26 1980 Nickel	N/A	0.2054 (1.356)
D22 1973 Molybdenum	N/A	0.1919 (-1.266)
D23 1974 Molybdenum	N/A	-0.0518 (-0.341)
R-Square	0.6190	0.9295
F-Statistic	16.973 (18,159)	94.342 (25,152)
Durbin-Watson	1.261	1.541

SOURCES: Dealer prices, *Metals Week* (various issues), IBRD, *Commodity Trade and Price Trends* (1986); Producer prices for aluminum, copper, lead and zinc, Standard and Poor's Corporation, *Basic Statistics on Metals, 1984,* and U.S. Bureau of Mines, ***Mineral Commodity*** *Summaries 1988,* for molybdenum and nickel, Amax Corporation.

* statistically significant

Appendix D

CALCULATION OF THE MARKET MODEL RESIDUALS

Residuals from the market model can be used to evaluate firm-specific performance, both over a period of time and cross-sectionally, of a stock price relative to the market. An individual company price would change with respect to that company's competitive position, while the market relative price would not.

Description

The relative value in the stock market of individual firms is determined by using the market model. In the market model the individual firm returns are regressed on the equally weighted market index of returns compiled by the Center for Research in Security Prices (University of Chicago).[1] Returns are defined as the change in price plus dividends in a year. Thus the relationship between the market returns and individual firm returns can be expressed as:

$$R_{it} = A + B_i R_{mt} + e_{it}$$

---

[1]For a detailed discussion of the market model and its underlying assumptions refer to Chapter 3 of *Foundations of Finance* by Eugene Fama. A detailed analysis of the event study methodology and the calculation of the market model residuals and the cumulative residuals is done in "Adjustment of Shock Prices to New Information" by Fama, Fisher, Jensen and Roll (1969).

where

R_{it} = Returns for firm i in period t
R_{mt} = Return for the equally weighted market index
A = Market model intercept
B_i = Systematic risk of security i
e_{it} = Market model residual.

It is assumed that e_{it} has a normal distribution with a mean zero and a variance $s^2(e_{it})$.

Here the market model is interpreted as consisting of more than just a statistical relation. The return on the equally weighted market portfolio (R_{mt}) is assumed to reflect the effects of all the variables on the returns of most of the securities. The residual e_{it} is presumed to capture the effects of the variables that are firm-specific. Thus in the market model, securities returns are caused by market factors b_iR_{mt}, and the remaining firm-specific factors e_{it}. The residuals e_{it} provide for the analyst a measure not of the effects of the marketwide factors on returns, but of the effects of company-specific conditions.

Results

Table Twenty-Two compares the performance for three firms and the metals industry as a whole from 1975 through 1986. Alcan is the largest aluminum-producing firm in North America, INCO is the largest nickel-producing firm in the world, and Amax is the world's largest molybdenum producer. The "metals industry" consists of an equally weighted portfolio of all the firms on the New York Stock Exchange and the American Stock Exchange that are listed as metals producers (the firms that have the Standard Industrial Classification Code of 3310 or 3370 are included). The equally weighted portfolio of the metals industry thus constructed has a total of 28,265 monthly stock returns.

The monthly returns for the four individual firms and the portfolio of the metals-producing firms, from January 1965 to December 1974, are regressed on the equally weighted market index for the same period. The estimated values of the alpha and beta coefficients for the individual firms and the metals industry are shown in Table D.1. The beta value for the three firms is less than 1.0, indicating that they are less risky than the total market. The beta coefficient for the metals industry is greater than 1.0, which implies a higher than total market risk for the industry (the inclusion of smaller firms may have caused the portfolio's risk factor to increase).[1]

The estimated alpha and beta coefficient values are used to calculate the monthly market model residuals from January 1975 to December 1986 for the individual companies and the portfolio of metals firms. The log value of 1.0 plus the monthly abnormal return is then added for each 36-month period in Table Twenty-Two. The exponential of this summed value for the 36-month period gives the cumulative value of the firm's abnormal return. The cumulative residuals are a measure of firm-specific performance as shown in Table D.2. They suggest that the larger firms were generally performing better than the overall metals industry during the estimation period.

An important assumption underlying the results is that the values of the alpha and beta coefficients are constant. In order to test this assumption, we estimated the market model coefficients for five-year periods from 1965 through 1984. The coefficient values from the different five-year market models from 1965 through 1984 were found to be reasonably stationary across the study period.

[1] For a discussion of the comparative risk of market model coefficients for small and large firms, refer to Chapter 4 of *Foundations of Finance* by Eugene Fama.

Table D.1. **Market Model for Individual Metal Firms and the Industry**

Independent Variable	*Alcan*	*Amax*	*INCO*	*Metal Industry*
		(Shown in percentage)		
Intercept	0.001	0.005	0.000	0.004
Market Return	0.838	0.761	0.941	1.1432
Period	1965-74	1965-74	1965-74	1965-74
Number of Observations	120	120	120	120

Table D.2. Cumulative Market Model Residuals for Metal Producing Firms

Period	*Alcan*	*Alcoa*	*Asarco*	*Amax*	*Phelps Dodge*	*INCO*	*US Steel*	*Metal Industries*
				$[e_{it} = R_{it} - (A_i + B_i R_{mt})]$ (*Shown in percentage*)				
1975	1.08%	33.70%	2.71%	59.63%	32.17%	25.17%	79.46%	-7.92%
1976	23.77	52.16	33.24	30.66	20.07	35.55	19.75	4.33
1977	16.10	-15.71	-6.73	-36.84	-44.48	-44.82	-32.78	-6.06
1978	36.29	6.99	-5.02	41.05	0.42	-3.79	-28.34	-2.40
1979	46.47	20.74	183.86	47.01	53.92	54.62	-11.26	7.46
1980	48.12	14.26	20.74	-5.00	27.23	-11.63	52.84	-12.76
1981	-26.02	-8.53	-38.08	20.35	-6.65	-27.83	29.23	5.76
1982	29.61	28.98	15.58	-52.48	-15.37	-15.95	-23.68	-28.63
1983	46.28	49.27	4.17	10.05	-10.22	26.24	50.43	9.52
1984	-24.65	-14.75	-35.95	-30.94	-45.04	-13.89	-10.68	-21.25
1985	5.19	7.79	-3.29	-15.67	65.77	8.70	5.97	-20.39
1986	-0.03	-9.19	-19.05	-11.01	-9.78	-9.97	-14.59	-21.75

SOURCE: Data obtained from Center for Research in Security Prices (University of Chicago).

NOTES: The cumulative market model residuals are calculated by using the market model for each firm. See Appendix D for methodology. The cumulative returns are continuously compounded for the twelve 12-month periods by adding the natural log of $(1 + e_{it})$ and then taking the exponential of the summed value, this process gives one plus the abnormal returns for the period. Then one is subtracted from the value to arrive at the continuously compounded abnormal returns.

Appendix E

DATA SERIES

Tables E.1 through E.8 contain the data used to calculate the various price level and dynamic equations. In each of the tables, the sources of the data set are given. The following is a list of the sources used:

American Bureau of Metals Statistics, Inc. *Non-Ferrous Metals Data.* New York: American Bureau of Metal Statistics, various issues.

International Bank for Reconstruction and Development. *Commodity Trade and Price Trends.* Washington, D.C.: IBRD, 1984 and 1986.

Metallgesellschaft A.G. *Metal Statistics.* Frankfurt am Main: MAG:,various years.

Standard and Poor's Corporation. *Basic Statistics on Metals.* New York: S&P, 1984.

United Nations. *Monthly Bulletin of Statistics.* New York: U.N., various issues.

United States Bureau of Mines. *Minerals Yearbook.* Washington, D.C.: Department of the Interior, various years.

United States Bureau of Mines. *Mineral Commodity Summaries.* Washington, D.C.,: Department of the Interior, 1984, 1985, 1987 and 1988.

Dimensions of all data are as follows: Prices are in dollars per pound; production, capacity, world stocks and exchange rates are indexed to the year 1980; and, also industrial production (GNP) and the wholesale price index are indexed to the year 1980.

Table E.1. Aluminum

Year	*Producer Price*	*Dealer Price*	*World Production*	*World Capacity*	*World Stocks*	*Producer Exchange Rate*
1960	27.23	23.00	28.28	40.46	160.69	1.06856
1961	25.46	21.00	27.54	41.98	373.53	1.08469
1962	23.88	20.00	30.19	43.51	298.75	1.09243
1963	22.62	20.00	33.18	44.27	201.67	1.06500
1964	23.72	22.00	37.46	46.56	142.51	1.06777
1965	24.50	22.00	39.91	48.85	139.33	1.07034
1966	24.50	22.00	43.83	50.38	93.21	1.07596
1967	13.98	22.00	48.22	54.96	107.73	1.07716
1968	25.58	21.00	51.48	61.07	315.12	1.09433
1969	27.18	26.00	58.38	63.36	102.07	1.09285
1970	28.72	25.00	63.13	70.99	61.86	1.10879
1971	29.00	20.00	67.26	83.21	201.80	1.14934
1972	26.67	20.00	71.94	89.31	257.72	1.10818
1973	25.33	30.00	79.16	90.46	172.72	1.06201
1974	34.06	43.00	86.29	91.60	89.24	1.06695
1975	39.79	31.00	77.32	91.60	132.81	1.07079
1976	44.49	39.00	79.65	93.13	206.53	1.07709
1977	51.35	45.00	88.11	94.66	153.20	1.05040
1978	54.42	48.00	90.33	95.42	165.41	1.00195
1979	61.01	69.64	92.70	96.95	135.45	0.99880
1980	70.87	78.64	100.00	100.00	100.00	1.00000
1981	77.19	61.00	97.53	102.29	137.16	1.04102
1982	76.38	48.00	84.25	109.16	205.61	1.11729
1983	77.53	68.00	86.89	113.74	193.80	1.12965
1984	81.00	64.00	99.95	116.03	133.60	1.16971
1985	81.00	50.00	95.82	118.05	114.00	1.10190
1986	81.00	50.00	94.35	120.00	95.00	1.06220

Table E.2. Copper

Year	*Producer Price*	*Dealer Price*	*World Production*	*World Capacity*	*World Stocks*	*Producer Exchange Rate*
1960	32.16	31.00	58.88	56.84	36.36	1.14871
1961	30.15	29.00	60.63	59.32	53.09	1.14647
1962	30.83	29.00	62.11	60.54	51.16	1.09622
1963	30.83	29.00	63.14	61.26	59.11	1.15473
1964	32.18	44.00	67.83	63.08	58.46	1.16017
1965	35.02	59.00	71.13	68.06	40.07	1.15281
1966	35.83	70.00	72.98	71.09	48.22	0.94719
1967	37.92	52.00	67.26	73.70	44.54	0.94102
1968	41.17	56.00	76.03	83.53	40.65	1.19692
1969	47.43	67.00	82.52	89.83	46.25	0.95822
1970	58.07	64.00	86.74	91.77	47.27	0.96168
1971	52.09	49.00	82.05	99.36	59.47	0.94910
1972	51.28	49.00	89.78	99.78	58.92	0.92728
1973	59.30	81.00	93.90	104.57	70.45	0.91082
1974	77.06	94.00	96.69	105.24	49.37	0.90592
1975	64.72	56.00	88.11	105.54	97.56	0.90309
1976	69.46	64.00	93.44	105.97	185.60	0.93358
1977	66.49	60.00	96.73	106.03	197.38	0.96286
1978	72.38	62.00	98.17	106.48	207.51	0.95484
1979	91.80	90.00	99.93	105.51	162.58	0.98675
1980	102.20	99.00	100.00	100.00	100.00	1.00000
1981	85.59	79.00	103.53	100.90	90.49	1.00848
1982	74.56	67.00	100.58	102.04	95.69	1.15461
1983	78.18	72.00	103.26	102.69	147.84	1.27954
1984	72.07	63.00	101.75	110.59	138.99	1.48912
1985	69.00	63.00	103.11	97.67	100.00	1.68770
1986	68.00	63.00	105.24	98.29	88.00	1.80820

Table E.3. Lead

Year	*Producer Price*	*Dealer Price*	*World Production*	*World Capacity*	*World Stocks*	*Producer Exchange Rate*
1960	11.75	9.00	45.15	64.52		1.17349
1961	10.70	8.00	46.46	64.52	99.56	1.13695
1962	9.43	7.00	45.62	67.74	128.76	1.16513
1963	10.94	8.00	48.00	67.74	104.14	1.17386
1964	13.42	13.00	49.17	67.74	176.69	1.16778
1965	15.80	14.00	51.35	74.19	80.61	1.16462
1966	14.92	12.00	53.32	80.65	79.52	1.17668
1967	13.80	10.00	53.61	80.65	80.17	1.22119
1968	13.01	11.00	56.75	83.87	100.00	1.18335
1969	14.73	13.00	64.34	90.32	73.64	1.26000
1970	15.49	14.00	66.04	93.55	90.20	1.26052
1971	13.69	12.00	63.01	93.55	108.93	1.22757
1972	15.34	14.00	64.36	93.55	104.36	1.15604
1973	16.31	20.00	66.49	93.55	102.40	1.02370
1974	22.49	27.00	65.51	90.32	81.70	1.02733
1975	21.48	19.00	83.50	90.32	113.94	1.07208
1976	23.10	20.00	93.03	90.32	125.71	1.10615
1977	30.72	28.00	98.76	93.55	100.44	1.09339
1978	33.76	30.00	99.82	93.55	101.96	1.04031
1979	53.19	55.00	100.88	100.00	84.31	1.01724
1980	42.91	41.18	100.00	100.00	100.00	1.00000
1981	37.11	33.00	97.17	100.00	114.38	1.05469
1982	26.03	25.00	94.38	96.77	112.85	1.12449
1983	26.00	19.00	94.70	100.00	122.00	1.15566
1984	26.50	20.00	94.88	103.23	117.65	1.22223
1985	20.00	19.00	96.19	100.00	91.00	1.07060
1986	22.00	19.00	96.90	100.00	76.00	1.01520

Table E.4. Nickel

Year	*Producer Price*	*World Production*	*World Capacity*	*World Stocks*	*Producer Exchange Rate*
1960	74.00	45.92	41.56		0.89019
1961	78.00	49.66	42.26		0.91978
1962	80.00	45.96	42.45		0.94236
1963	79.00	46.77	42.64		0.95981
1964	79.00	50.27	44.73		0.96620
1965	79.00	57.59	47.91	88.14	0.95506
1966	79.00	54.75	50.51	71.75	0.96302
1967	88.00	58.05	52.22	159.89	0.96246
1968	94.00	66.25	54.89	158.76	0.97197
1969	105.00	62.42	60.85	140.68	1.01608
1970	129.00	86.92	71.64	84.75	1.00594
1971	133.00	84.99	79.95	126.55	0.96233
1972	140.00	85.56	80.52	84.49	0.91608
1973	153.00	97.76	81.85	134.46	0.89911
1974	174.00	109.98	88.52	147.46	0.91514
1975	207.00	111.10	94.29	232.20	0.90829
1976	225.00	111.30	96.38	181.36	0.91291
1977	241.00	113.10	97.21	162.15	0.97301
1978	205.00	83.22	97.97	95.48	0.97340
1979	275.00	87.46	99.62	104.52	1.00384
1980	341.00	100.00	100.00	100.00	1.00000
1981	343.00	90.36	99.56	71.19	1.07358
1982	320.00	80.16	104.44	118.08	1.19665
1983	320.00	83.81	105.90	96.61	1.29383
1984	320.00	92.69	104.19	107.34	1.32683
1985	201.00	98.17	101.27	117.36	1.33660
1986	320.00	87.64	98.97	103.31	1.36210

Table E.5. Molybdenum

Year	*Producer Price*	*World Production*	*World Capacity*	*World Stocks*	*Producer Exchange Rate*
1960	147.00	35.01	28.36		0.95327
1961	155.00	34.63	28.36	45.83	0.95290
1962	160.00	27.45	21.45	43.08	0.92195
1963	160.00	35.15	27.27	29.17	0.90431
1964	171.00	36.46	28.36	34.72	0.88390
1965	175.00	46.11	28.36	33.33	0.89795
1966	175.00	58.50	36.00	40.28	0.89020
1967	181.00	59.17	43.64	70.83	0.88333
1968	182.00	59.94	46.55	95.83	0.90969
1969	189.00	66.76	52.00	98.61	0.91237
1970	192.00	75.41	61.82	102.78	0.89361
1971	192.00	70.18	61.82	138.89	0.87755
1972	192.00	73.49	61.82	168.06	0.88018
1973	192.00	75.88	61.82	173.61	0.88444
1974	230.00	77.77	61.82	151.39	0.83598
1975	262.00	73.35	65.45	136.11	0.85691
1976	345.00	81.84	69.09	130.56	0.87313
1977	401.00	88.14	72.73	122.22	0.92002
1978	495.00	90.99	80.00	119.44	0.96355
1979	750.00	94.75	80.00	112.50	0.99023
1980	970.00	100.00	100.00	100.00	1.00000
1981	850.00	98.19	109.09	151.36	1.01621
1982	400.00	89.11	120.00	205.56	1.21219
1983	365.00	49.19	120.00	251.39	1.98807
1984	340.00	82.96	120.00	201.39	2.06897
1985	330.00	85.75	120.00	150.00	4.74900
1986	314.00	75.82	94.23	65.00	4.52720

Table E.6. Steel

Year	*Producer Price*	*World Stocks*	*Producer Exchange Rate*
1960	6.00	51.82	1.25705
1961	5.00	53.30	1.25754
1962	5.00	53.42	1.25418
1963	6.00	57.77	1.23764
1964	6.00	66.98	1.24545
1965	6.00	69.69	1.24116
1966	6.00	71.28	1.24854
1967	6.00	74.46	1.28016
1968	6.00	79.99	1.30027
1969	7.00	88.12	1.30342
1970	7.00	90.31	1.29065
1971	8.00	85.15	1.26400
1972	8.00	93.40	1.18486
1973	9.00	105.57	1.11637
1974	12.00	106.34	1.19133
1975	13.00	91.06	1.13840
1976	13.00	97.41	1.14734
1977	15.00	94.74	1.09084
1978	17.00	100.00	0.98513
1979	18.00	106.37	0.98711
1980	21.00	100.00	1.00000
1981	23.00	99.04	1.03589
1982	24.00	85.63	1.11872
1983	26.00	87.41	1.11244
1984	27.00	89.00	1.15649
1985	28.00	86.00	1.00780
1986	25.00	84.00	0.86990

Table E.7. Zinc

Year	*Producer Price*	*Dealer Price*	*World Production*	*World Capacity*	*World Stocks*	*Producer Exchange Rate*
1960	12.96	11.00	53.84	51.72	52.67	1.30283
1961	11.55	10.00	57.35	53.45	53.42	1.29683
1962	11.63	8.00	59.15	59.90	53.85	1.28256
1963	12.01	10.00	61.07	59.90	57.45	1.17065
1964	13.57	15.00	66.02	60.34	57.33	1.18426
1965	14.50	14.00	69.67	65.52	47.12	1.17915
1966	14.50	13.00	73.31	68.97	46.88	1.19360
1967	13.85	12.00	72.78	74.14	52.04	1.20533
1968	13.50	12.00	80.98	74.14	55.41	1.22724
1969	14.65	13.00	88.10	77.59	57.57	1.23666
1970	15.32	13.00	89.11	77.59	54.33	1.25959
1971	16.14	14.00	84.21	81.03	62.38	1.23973
1972	17.72	17.00	93.05	84.48	81.97	1.17275
1973	20.26	39.00	95.51	87.93	73.80	1.08058
1974	35.94	56.00	94.85	87.93	70.31	1.17620
1975	38.90	34.00	83.38	89.66	55.05	1.15697
1976	37.45	32.00	91.67	91.38	91.23	1.11295
1977	34.38	27.00	94.73	96.55	137.74	1.11278
1978	31.14	27.00	95.33	98.28	137.14	0.98388
1979	38.86	34.00	104.66	98.28	143.63	0.99340
1980	38.03	35.00	100.00	100.00	100.00	1.00000
1981	45.42	38.00	101.67	100.00	104.45	1.03566
1982	40.24	34.00	96.74	101.72	94.59	1.11468
1983	43.02	35.00	103.91	105.17	105.17	1.12738
1984	50.00	42.00	108.71	108.62	96.27	1.16667
1985	42.00	33.00	111.46	113.61	77.00	1.15390
1986	41.00	35.00	108.86	117.48	78.00	1.00840

Table E.8. Other Data

Year	*Industrial GNP*	*Wholesale Price Index*
1960	40.7	26
1961	42.6	26
1962	45.4	27
1963	48.0	27
1964	51.8	28
1965	55.2	29
1966	59.0	30
1967	60.5	31
1968	64.5	32
1969	70.5	33
1970	71.2	34
1971	74.2	36
1972	79.3	38
1973	86.2	43
1974	87.2	52
1975	81.4	57
1976	88.5	63
1977	92.1	69
1978	95.7	74
1979	100.4	85
1980	100.0	100
1981	100.1	113
1982	97.6	125
1983	100.6	139
1984	104.9	160
1985	106.3	171
1986	108.1	182

INDEX

GPSR Compliance

The European Union's (EU) General Product Safety Regulation (GPSR) is a set of rules that requires consumer products to be safe and our obligations to ensure this.

If you have any concerns about our products, you can contact us on ProductSafety@springernature.com

In case Publisher is established outside the EU, the EU authorized representative is:

Springer Nature Customer Service Center GmbH
Europaplatz 3
69115 Heidelberg, Germany

Batch number: 10823771

Printed by Printforce, the Netherlands